FROM DIPLOMAS TO DOCTORATES

FROM DIPLOMAS TO DOCTORATES

The Success of Black Women in Higher Education
and Its Implications for Equal Educational
Opportunities for All

Edited by V. Barbara Bush,
Crystal Renée Chambers,
and MaryBeth Walpole

Foreword by Kassie Freeman
Afterword by Wynetta Y. Lee

STERLING, VIRGINIA

COPYRIGHT © 2009 BY
STYLUS PUBLISHING, LLC.

Published by Stylus Publishing, LLC
22883 Quicksilver Drive
Sterling, Virginia 20166-2102

Library of Congress Cataloging-in-Publication-Data
From diplomas to doctorates : the success of black women in higher education and its implications for equal educational opportunities for all / edited by V. Barbara Bush, Crystal Gafford Muhammad, and MaryBeth Walpole ; foreword by Kassie Freeman ; afterword by Wynetta Y. Lee.
    p.   cm.
Includes bibliographical references and index.
ISBN 978-1-57922-356-4 (cloth : alk. paper)
ISBN 978-1-57922-357-1 (pbk. : alk. paper)
1. African American women—Education (Higher)
2. Doctor of philosophy degree—United States.   3. African American women—Social conditions.   4. Discrimination in higher education—United States.   5. Educational equalization.   I. Bush, V. Barbara.   II. Gafford Muhammad, Crystal   III. Walpole, MaryBeth, 1960–
LC2781.F77   2010
378.1'9822—dc22

                           2009052928

13-digit ISBN: 978-1-57922-356-4 (cloth)
13-digit ISBN: 978-1-57922-357-1 (paper)

Printed in the United States of America

All first editions printed on acid free paper
that meets the American National Standards Institute
Z39-48 Standard.

Bulk Purchases

Quantity discounts are available for use in workshops and for staff development.
Call 1-800-232-0223

First Edition, 2009

10   9   8   7   6   5   4   3   2   1

This volume outlines many of the struggles, challenges, celebrations, and victories of African Americans who traveled that unpaved road from diplomas to doctorates. The expectation is that these "successful" women will not be selfish with their rewards, but will instead lift as they climb, becoming role models and mentors for all who follow. This volume is dedicated to you.

CONTENTS

PART THREE: THE GRADUATE EXPERIENCE

LIST OF FIGURES AND TABLES

Introduction

Chapter 1

Chapter 2

FOREWORD

When it comes to underrepresented groups in education at any level, there is no room for *either/or*. In the case of African Americans, neither women nor men have reached their full potential. Therefore, there is room for improvement for men and women.

Black women outnumber men in enrollment in higher education institutions. Yet, Black women face challenges just as Black men do in participation in, graduation from, and their work in educational institutions compared to their White counterparts. Therefore, there is no reason for all attention to be turned to Black men, while losing sight of the challenges confronting Black women.

As pointed out in this highly important book, Black women students confront challenges at each step along the educational continuum and in each higher education institution type. Often, however, research and scholarship on Black women is somehow isolated or marginalized, which enables the protracted challenges confronting Black women to grow rather than abate.

What makes this book important is that it highlights some of the challenges facing Black women at various steps along the education pipeline and enhances the discussions about the educational dilemmas Black women face. Why will it not be another book tossed aside as "Black feminists at it again, promoting their agenda"? What new and insightful additions will it add to scholarly discussions in education arenas/circles? These are legitimate questions and merit responses before reading this book.

First, even if it were a book written solely from a Black feminist theoretical perspective, that would be neither inappropriate nor bad. However, this book has as its basis higher education and sociological theoretical underpinnings. Written from the perspective of new and seasoned voices in the field, this volume brings an air of freshness and excitement to this topic, unlike other books.

Next, unlike previous research and books that examine the status and condition of Black women along the education pipeline, this book takes a snapshot of Black women's experiences holistically. For example, books such as *Spirit, Space & Survival: African American Women in (White) Academe* (1993) edited by James and Farmer; Hull, Bell Scott, and Smith's *All the Women Are White, All the Blacks Are Men, But Some of Us Are Brave: Black Women's Studies* (1982); and *Gender Talk: The Struggle for Women's Equality in African American Communities* (2003) by Cole and Guy-Sheftall are all excellent and necessary reading to set the foundation for understanding the overall status of women in the academy. However, these books leave an opening for a work, like this one, to address the dilemmas that Black women have confronted and continue to confront during their progression along the higher education pipeline that have led to their status in the academy and in the larger society in the first place. Last, far from promoting an agenda, this book is based on solid research with the intent to confront Black women's educational dilemmas squarely, and it ends with programmatic recommendations to address their dilemmas. Therefore, this book is written from a much broader theoretical perspective than, say, a feminist perspective.

What new and insightful additions will this book bring to scholarly discussions? The range and depth of topics this book explores are groundbreaking and insightful. There is no doubt that, when the topic of Black women in higher education is explored, this book will be one of the first to be highlighted. There will not be many other books to compare with the sheer range of necessary topics related to the issues facing Black women explored here.

Next, the fact that this book does not limit itself to any one methodological paradigm certainly will add to scholarly discussions. Obviously, the editors have intentionally selected researchers who bring quantitative, qualitative, and/or historical methods together to address this topic.

Another aspect in which this book will add to scholarly discussion is the way in which these chapters do not limit themselves to institution types or experiences. Rather, the chapter authors build on each other to demonstrate Black women's experiences in different institutions, settings, and dilemmas.

Ultimately, though, you, as the reader, must judge for yourself. As Janie, the heroine in Zora Neale Hurston's book, *Their Eyes Were Watching God* (1937/2006), states: "Two things everybody's got tu do fur theyselves. They got tuh go tuh God, and they got tuh find out about livin' fuh theyselves" (p. 192).

I invite you to read this book and find out for yourself. There will be much to bring you to *From Diplomas to Doctorates* as a source on the experiences of Black women in education many times over.

Kassie Freeman
Interim President
Southern University System

References

Cole, J. B., & Guy-Sheftall, B. (2003). *Gender talk: The struggle for women's equality in African American communities.* New York: Ballantine.

Hull, G. T., Bell Scott, P., & Smith, B. (Eds.) (1982). *All the women are White, all the Blacks are men, but some of us are brave: Black women's studies.* New York: The Feminist Press.

Hurston, Z. N. (1937/2006). *Their eyes were watching God.* New York: Harper.

James, J., & Farmer, R. (1993). *Spirit, space & survival: African American women in (white) academe.* New York: Routledge.

INTRODUCTION

Crystal Renée Chambers, V. Barbara Bush,
and MaryBeth Walpole

ull, Bell Scott, and Smith advocated for Black women's studies in
*All the Women Are White, All the Blacks Are Men, But Some of Us
Are Brave: Black Women's Studies* (1982). Within that same spirit
this volume acknowledges that the influences of race, class, and gender on
everyday life are nonlinear. Whereas contemporary Black women are comparatively more successful in educational attainment than their male counterparts, this success fails to negate the race, class, and gender burdens Black
women shoulder. Johnnetta B. Cole and Beverly Guy-Sheftall (2003) summa-
rized it best: "The popular notion that Black men are an 'endangered species'
has given the impression that all is well with Black women" (p. xxix). The
inherent problem with this perspective is that "this image of the endangered
Black male unfortunately reinforces the notion that improving the status of
Black men will single-handedly solve all the complex problems facing African American communities" (p. xxix).

Transitioning from the community at large to campus is often an isolating experience, regardless of previous academic successes. Being neither
White nor male raises the question of locating an African American woman's
space and place within the academy. In her thought-provoking essay, "Third
World Diva Girls: Politics of Feminist Solidarity," bell hooks (1990) spoke
of a Black woman graduate student who tried to engage a scholar whose
work analyzed the experiences of African American women:

> She . . . left this encounter feeling crushed, wondering why prominent
> black women scholars of all ethnicities rarely mentor black women stu-
> dents. How can prominent women of color engaged in [the] feminist

movement be surprised that there is so little participation in the
movement. . . . if we behave as though feminism is only for those of us
who are "special"? Or if we behave as though feminism is a turf we have
conquered, a field of power where we can maintain authority and presence,
and reap rewards only if there [are] a few of us present, if we are a rare
commodity. (pp. 100–101)

This student's encounter is grounded within a particular field of scholarly
endeavor—feminist theory—which, by definition, should have been an open
space and place for her. This ironic episode illustrates a larger issue within
the academy. Will we as members of the academy provide the support necessary for students to grow and thrive while traversing the diploma-to-doctorate
continuum?

This volume illuminates the educational experiences of Black women,
from high school diplomas through graduate study, exploring their unique
and non-unique paths and challenges. The perspectives in this volume are
theoretically grounded, and the methodologies used are diverse for the purposes of gaining a circumspect, in-depth understanding of the higher education experiences of Black women students. It answers a call for more research
on African American women in the academy (Haniff, 1991; Matthews &
Jackson, 1991) and extends as well as deepens the understandings of experiences presented in works such as *Black Women in the Academy: Promises and
Perils* (Benjamin, 1997), *Sisters of the Academy: Emergent Black Women Scholars in the Academy* (Mabokela & Green, 2001), and, most recently, *From
Oppression to Grace: Women of Color and Their Dilemmas within the Academy*
(Berry & Mizzelle, 2006).

As is the case with these works, the authors in this volume take an appre-
ciative approach to their data analyses. Too often, the focus of studies of
nondominant groups in education centers on the perceived deficits of these
students—deficits that imply lack of social and cultural capital based on
prior educational experiences, socioeconomic status, race, and gender. We
believe that the perspective of a deficit model is detrimental, not only to the
student, but also to higher education in general. The field of higher education, and the nation more broadly, lose when there is a failure to appreciate
the skills and talents that arrive at the ivory tower gate. Too often too many
students are misread—books misjudged by their covers. Thus, we believe
that by focusing on strengths, we present a research perspective that promotes strengthening the academic pipeline, not only to help those who may

have felt disenfranchised in the past, but also to promote more globally defined collective self-interests.

Before we delve into the research our contributors have provided, we the editors provide a historic and statistical overview of the educational trajectories of African American women beyond the diploma. From there we present a synthesis of the chapters following the educational paths of Black women from their high school diplomas and decisions to attend college through their doctoral degree process.

While the educational paths taken are many, we are most interested in the paths to the doctorate, as this particular degree is crucial to the faculty and to positions of higher education leadership. Our goal is to provide snapshots along the diploma-to-doctorate continuum where we as faculty can be particularly attuned to support our sisters. In addition, we hope this work is helpful for students in spotlighting pitfalls and noting pragmatic tips for traversing their process successfully. While we write regarding the specific experiences of African American women, these works collectively are useful in guiding students who are also marginalized by dominant society. Ultimately, the case built in *From Diplomas to Doctorates* is that the strategies African American women use to rise, survive, and thrive demonstrate resilience and strength from which *all* students can benefit.

The Educational Trajectory of African American Women: A Longitudinal Analysis

State law often prohibited the education of early African Americans generally, and most specifically those enslaved in the South (Anderson, 1988). However, because these laws did not eradicate the thirst to learn, even in colonial America some intellectuals of African descent, including Benjamin Banneker and Phillis Wheatley, found ways to become educated (Renfro, 1993). Further, despite laws curtailing educational content and delivery to persons of African descent, as early as the 1840s Black women began making their way to American colleges and universities. Oberlin College was among the first to admit students of African descent. Bauman (2002) reports Sarah J. Watson Barnett as the first Black woman to enroll at Oberlin in 1842. In 1850, Lucy Stanton was the first to obtain a bachelor's degree (Bauman, 2002). As reported by W. E. B. DuBois (1900), before 1880, 54 African American women graduated from 10 U.S. colleges and universities, at least

10 of whom graduated before the Civil War. Thirty-one of these women graduated from Oberlin College in Ohio. DuBois recounted several of their experiences. Here are but a few:

- I was born in a farm in Ohio, and lived there until I was sixteen. My father died when I was twelve and I had to provide for myself. At the age of sixteen I taught a country school and saved $100. With this I went to Oberlin; and went through by teaching and working.
- Was born and schooled in Philadelphia during the dark days of slavery. Was intimately associated with the work of the Underground Railroad and the Anti-Slavery Society. I was sent to Oberlin in 1864.
- I went to school at Monroe, Michigan, until a female seminary was opened there, from which colored children were barred. I then went to Oberlin.
- My father was a Creole and my mother a free Negro woman. We moved from Mobile, Ala., to Wilberforce, O., where I was reared. My parents were devoted Christians, and were blessed with the comforts of life. My father had a fine collection of books.
- At a very early age I assumed the responsibility of housekeeper, as my mother died and I was the oldest of a family of five; hence I labored under the many disadvantages in attending school, but nevertheless I performed my household duties, persevered with my studies, and now I feel that I have been rewarded.
- My mother and I "took in" washing for our support and to enable me to get an education. After finishing the public schools of Jacksonville, Ill., I was supported four years in college by a scholarship. (pp. 53–54)

Disproportionately poor, although varied in socioeconomic status, these women were trailblazers, enrolling in U.S. colleges and universities at a time when higher educational opportunities for women and people of color in general were limited but expanding.

During this early era, African American women comprised only 10% of African American college graduates: 252 women, compared to 2,272 men (DuBois, 1900, p. 55). In addition, most African American women then attended predominantly White institutions (PWIs). However, by the 1940s, this trend had reversed. Historically Black colleges and universities (HBCUs) had grown in number, enrollment capacity, and educational scope. As pressures from the "cult of true womanhood" encouraged White women to withdraw and refrain from college (Perkins, 1983), African American women began to outpace both White women and Black men in their college participation and baccalaureate attainment rates. By 1940, African American women received 3,244 bachelor of arts degrees from the nation's HBCUs, compared to 2,463 bachelor of arts degrees earned by Black males. By the early 1950s, African American women had outpaced their male counterparts in acquiring the master's degree and received 66.4% of all degrees awarded by HBCUs. Male prominence in doctoral degrees, however, remained (Giddings, 1984/2006).

Newly secured freedoms in the post-Civil Rights Era were accompanied by increases in college enrollments of young Blacks, men and women alike (Anderson, 1988). According to U.S. Department of Education, National Center for Education Statistics (NCES) data (2003), by 1976, the number of African American women enrolled in postsecondary education was 563,100: 512,700 undergraduate students, 46,500 graduates, and 3,900 women working on their first professional degree. Unless otherwise stated, data throughout this analysis are from the U.S. Department of Education NCES *Digest of Education Statistics*, Tables 209 and 217 (2003, 2007), respectively. As depicted in Figure I.1, college enrollments among Black women continued to climb through the present era, skyrocketing in 1990. From 1976 to 1980, Black women's overall enrollment increased by 12.4%, the largest gains made by students pursuing first-time professional degrees (a 29% increase). Enrollment of undergraduate students during this period increased by 13.1%, while graduate enrollment moved upward by less than 1%. From 1980 to 1990, African American women's enrollment increased by 15.6%. Enrollment of African American women pursuing first-time professional degrees increased by 35.3%, while the increase in undergraduate enrollment was 15.5%. Increases in graduate enrollment during this period made considerable traction, gaining at a rate of 14%.

From 1990 to 2000, growth in the college enrollment of African American women spiked at 30.3%, bringing the number of African American women enrolled over the 1 million mark.[1] This increase was fueled largely by undergraduate enrollment, with over 272,500 more African American women joining the undergraduate ranks, a 28% increase. Professional enrollments also increased by 39.2% to 8,500 students. Most impressive, graduate

FIGURE I.1
African American Women Enrollments, Select Years, 1976–2005

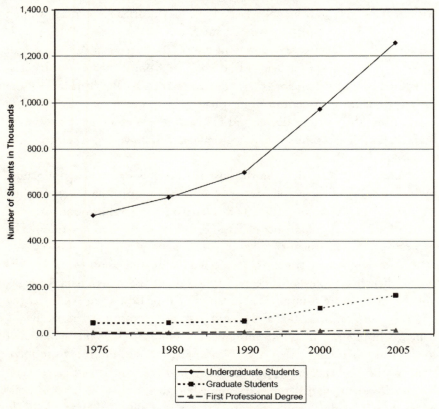

enrollment nearly doubled, from 54,600 graduate students in 1990 to 109,000 in 2000.

The enrollment of African American women continued to increase between 2000 and 2005, although at a slightly less aggressive rate of 23.9%. During this period, undergraduate enrollment alone totaled more than a million students, a 22.7% gain between 2000 and 2005. Graduate enrollments continued at a higher rate of growth, 34.5%. The rate of enrollment increases in first-time professional degree programs, however, tapered significantly, growing by only 13.5%. These most recent trends in enrollments are plotted year by year in Figure I.2.

FIGURE I.2
African American Women Enrollments, 2000–2005

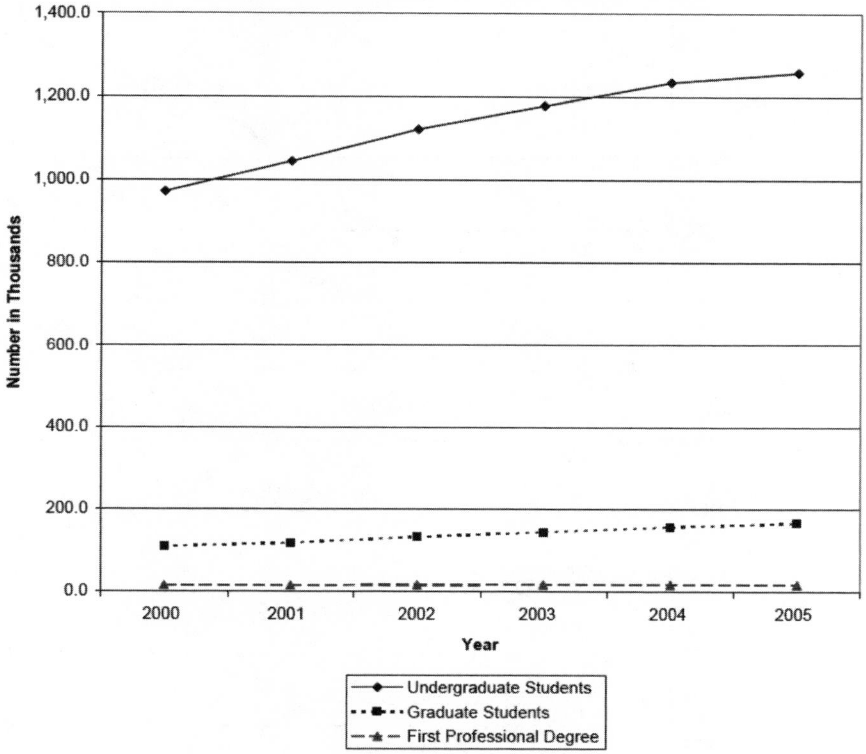

As displayed in Figure I.3, increases in degree attainment among African American women are similarly strong. At a time when overall bachelor's degree awards rose by 23%, from 1994–1995 to 2004–2005, the number of African American women attaining baccalaureate degrees increased by 66.8%, to 87,525. Master's degree attainment for African American women increased at a rate of 152.5%, to 35,304. Awards of professional degrees to African American women grew at a rate of 53.2%, to 3,846.

To understand the trajectories of these women toward the doctorate and into faculty and higher education leadership roles, it is also important to understand the fields in which African American women are earning their degrees. According to NCES (U.S. Department of Education, 2007), in 2005–2006

FIGURE I.3
African American Women's Degree Attainment, 1994–1995 to 2004–2005

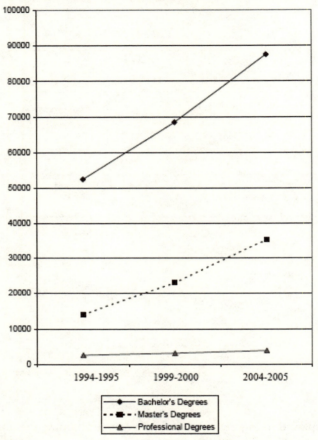

African American women earned their bachelor's degrees most often in the field of business. They earned law degrees most often as first professional degrees and chose education most often for master's and doctoral degrees.

Figure I.4 depicts increases in doctoral degree attainment among African American women from 1994–1995 to 2004–2005. During this period, overall doctoral degree attainments rose just over 20%, while the numbers in some groups, including White and Asian women, declined. The number of African American women completing their doctoral degrees, however, increased by 154.7% (Cook & Cordova, 2007).

FIGURE I.4
Doctoral Degree Attainment of African American Women, 1994–1995 to 2004–2005

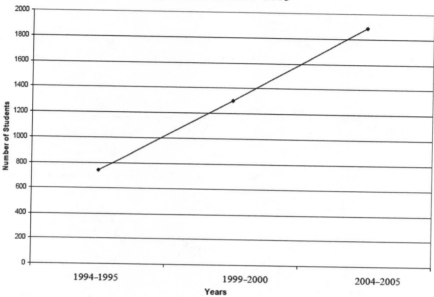

Increases in the number of African American women degree recipients seem to have translated into increases in African American women faculty over this same period, especially among the academy's lower ranks (see Figure I.5). Across the ranks, from 1995 to 2005, African American women increased their presence among full-time instructional faculty by 30%, to 18,429. The largest gains were made among lecturers and instructors, 40% and 35%, respectively. Sizable increases among "other" faculty were made as well: 32%. The number of African American women faculty in tenure-track positions appreciably grew as well. The number of assistant professors grew by 24%, to 5,438; the number of associate professors grew by 30%, to 3,455; and the number of full professors increased by 15%, to 1,986. These gains notwithstanding, data from a recent report, "The State of Blacks in Higher Education 2008" by Sharpe, Darity, and Swinton, indicate that Black women are generally more likely not to be retained in tenure-track positions. In fact, they are twice as likely as other faculty to switch from tenure tracks to adjunct positions (cited by Schmidt, 2008). This development has significant

FIGURE I.5
African American Women Faculty by Rank, 1995–2005

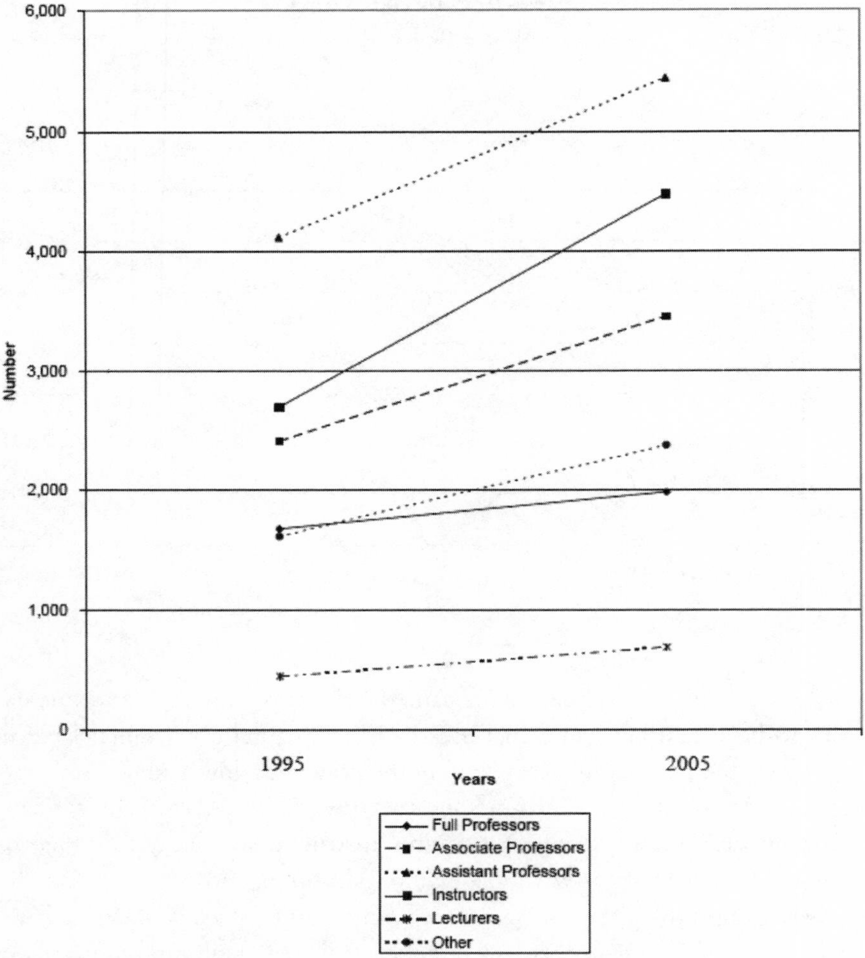

repercussions for African American women among the ranks of education leaders.

Increases in doctoral degree attainment have increased the number of African American women faculty. Yet, more doctorates do not seem to translate into greater numbers of African American women in higher education leadership positions, especially the presidency. Data from the American

Council on Education pertaining specifically to African American women were not available, but we do know that between 1986 and 2006, the number of African American college presidents, both men and women, increased only minimally—from 5% to 6%. Exacerbating this concern is the fact that nearly 50% of current college presidents are nearing retirement age (American Council on Education [ACE], 2007), and a new generation of African American administrators will be needed to fill some of these vacancies. Scholars in higher education have an opportunity to develop the future leadership of colleges and universities by supporting the movement of faculty into executive positions that constitute pathways to the presidency—positions such academic dean and vice president.

The need for a stronger pipeline from the doctorate to the presidency becomes evident when we examine the stagnant numbers of college presidents of African descent. Pipeline concerns are particularly acute in community colleges, where women presidents of all races and ethnicities constitute approximately 29% of campus leadership. According to a national survey of community college presidents, 56% planned to retire in 5 years, while 86% planned to do so in 10 years (American Association of Community Colleges [AACC], 2006). Vaughan and Weisman (1998), who studied community college presidents, posited that since 90% of current presidents held a doctorate, the lack of this terminal degree could be one of the major reasons African Americans were underrepresented in the presidency. As the number of African American women with doctorates grows, the hope is that we will see an increase in their representation, not only among faculty, but also in higher education administration.

While the growth in African American women's success along the diploma-to-doctorate continuum is laudable, it has not occurred without difficulty and has at times extracted an exacting toll. These women have succeeded despite racism and sexism. We hope to shed light here on how these women have succeeded, the routes they have taken, and how they have overcome racism and sexism. It is our hope that, not only other African American women, but also women and men from all races, ethnicities, and socioeconomic statuses, can learn and benefit from these experiences.

From Diplomas to Doctorates

Demographic data illustrate that once African American students enter college, more women persist to graduation than do men. Although it is evident that they persist, we need to study *how* they persist and what conditions may hinder these women from higher persistence. The chapters of this volume identify key spheres of influence for students, including access, transition, and experience factors as well as outcomes and pipelines. This volume presents empirical research on the higher education of African American women from college predisposition to undergraduate enrollment and baccalaureate attainment to the doctoral degree. It is divided into three parts: the precollegiate phase and transitions to college, undergraduate experiences, and the graduate experience, with a special focus on doctoral education. Using an array of inquiry methods, the authors consider the resilience of young Black women at each phase of education, from secondary through graduate school, highlighting successes with an eye toward learning from the challenges posed.

Part One: The Precollegiate and Transitional Experience

Part One begins with chapter 1, "College Predisposition and the Dilemma of Being Black and Female in High School" by Adrienne D. Dixson and Crystal Renée Chambers. Whereas Ferguson (2001) highlights the amount of negative attention that Black boys receive and how it discourages engagement with the educational process, the authors find that young Black women feel supported in their educational endeavors. Nevertheless, within their classrooms and school hallways, these women are witnesses to injustices to people who look like them in all aspects but gender. Data analysis using the Educational Longitudinal Survey of 2002 seems to indicate that young Black women are generally confused about how they assess an academic environment that may not be particularly hostile to them, but has the potential for being hostile to others. This hostility does not seem to impede their success; this does not mean, however, that they are not scarred in ways that are more difficult to quantify.

Chambers follows with chapter 2, "'Making a Dollar Out of Fifteen Cents': The Early Educational Investments of Young Black Women." In this chapter she explores the human, social, and cultural capital investments of young Black women using the fourth follow-up to the National Educational Longitudinal Survey of 1988 (NELS:88/00). Using binomial logistic analysis, Chambers isolates cultural capital factors that predict college enrollment for young Black women, but not young Black men. To underscore the resilience of young Black women, she compares their "baskets" of human, social, and cultural capital with those of the rest of the NELS:88/00 population and finds that, with the amount of capital they are given and actively acquire in their precollegiate years, young Black women gain greater returns on their educational investments than their male peers.

Part Two: The Undergraduate Experience

In chapter 3, Rachelle Winkle-Wagner explores how African American women students' peers support and inhibit their transition to college in "An Asset or an Obstacle? The Power of Peers in African American Women's College Transitions." With this qualitative study, using a critical ethnography approach, Winkle-Wagner poignantly illustrates the assistance and the interference African American women receive from their peers during their transition to college at one PWI. The students' peer interactions shape their early college experiences and influence subsequent persistence decisions.

Chapter 3 also serves as a transition from the precollegiate experiences of African American women to Part Two of this volume—the experiences of students during college. Leading off with chapter 4, "African American Female Students at Historically Black Colleges: Historical and Contemporary Considerations" by Marybeth Gasman investigates both the historical and contemporary experiences of Black women at HBCUs using gender as a lens. Gasman asserts that Black women's experiences at HBCUs have been under researched and that discussions of gender equity at HBCUs have been lacking as a consequence of a focus on racial equality. Her analysis traces Black women's experiences from the founding of HBCUs by White missionaries through the Civil Rights Movement to students' current experiences.

In chapter 5, "African American Women at Highly Selective Colleges: How African American Campus Communities Shape Experiences," Mary-Beth Walpole examines African American women's experiences at two highly selective PWIs and explores the role of African American campus communities in those experiences. Her qualitative study incorporates a Bourdieuian framework to illustrate how race, social class, and gender shape students' cultural capital and habitus, which, in turn, mediate their campus experiences. Her analysis also illuminates three roles that African American campus communities play. They are: (1) a haven from an isolating and racist campus; (2) a conduit for social capital accumulation; and (3) a site for middle- and upper-middle-class African American culture accumulation.

Part Three: The Graduate Experience

Part Three begins with chapter 6, "Professional Socialization, Politicized, Raced and Gendered Experience, and Black Female Graduate Students: A Road Map for Structural Transformation." In this study Venice Thandi Sulé explores how Black female graduate students are socialized into the academic profession as graduate students at selective PWIs. Given the significance of race and gender discrimination within higher education and the relatively low numbers of Black female professors, compared to the number of Black women students, this exploratory study examines how Black women in the social and natural sciences navigate through this often rocky terrain. Informed by Black feminist thought and political race theory, Sulé finds that, rather than experiencing positive professional socialization, Black females are expected to accept their subordinate status through organizational acculturation—the process of adopting the norms and values of the dominant group. This position of subordination postures dissonantly with their sense of self-worth, which, in turn, fosters resistance and oppositional knowledge. In this posture, Black women are like miner's canaries, the first exposed to race- and gender-biased toxins in the academic environment. Sulé argues that because of this posturing, the oppositional knowledge developed can be the exact prescription needed to alleviate racism and sexism on campus.

In chapter 7, "Does Where They Start Matter? A Comparative Analysis of African American Women Doctoral Recipients Who Started in a Two-Year Versus a Four-Year Institution," Carolyn Buck addresses the fact that a strikingly large number of African American women access postsecondary education at community colleges: 11% of all African American women with doctorates start at the community college, yet, the two-year institution is rarely studied as a pathway to the doctorate. In a comparative analysis, she addresses the vacuum in the literature regarding community colleges and terminal degree acquisition. Her study compares African American doctoral recipients whose point of entry was a two-year college with doctoral recipients whose point of entry was a four-year college. She finds that while the women who began at two-year colleges were better able than their peers to limit the amount of their student loan debt, given their point of entry, these women needed more mentoring and advising support than did their counterparts who began at four-year institutions to ensure successful college transfer and student persistence to the terminal degree. Moreover, the sheer volume of African American women starting higher education at community colleges warrants closer attention to the skill sets of students beginning there to identify those who may wish pursue a doctorate.

In the final chapter, "A Look Back and a Look Ahead: How to Navigate the Doctoral Degree Process Successfully," Benita J. Barnes uses autoethnography to examine doctoral education from the perspectives of a doctoral student herself and as a faculty member mentoring doctoral students. Throughout this autoethnography, her research in the field renders her analysis particularly insightful, providing researchers and graduate students alike with rich information on how to engage and succeed in the doctoral process.

Conclusion

Given the history of higher education from its European and American colonial origins, most U.S. colleges and universities are imbued with androcentric and Eurocentric norms. As such, nonmale, non-White entrants to the academy have often found the climate at PWIs beyond "chilly," to cold, brutal, and harsh. While the experience of inhospitable campuses is not exclusive to African American women, by virtue of women's multiplicative marginalized identities, these campus climates render them particularly excludable for reasons of their race, gender, and, often, class.

The editors and authors of *From Diplomas to Doctorates* believe that African American women bring to the college campus significant cultural and social capital gained from life experience. This precollege capital includes resilience, a strong history of overcoming obstacles, healthy self-esteem, and proven coping strategies based on religious affiliation, parental factors, educational experience, peers, role models, and community support. However, where precollege capital is weak, African American women can gain strength through their engagement within the educational community through peers, faculty, and mentors. They can also grow from the inside out toward an increasing sense of self. Finally, the consistent theme throughout this volume is that Black women use many pathways to gain this strength. Their successes in doing so are evident across multiple domains in the higher education sector: two-year and four-year institutions, PWIs, and HBCUs.

In a 2002 interview with *Black Issues in Higher Education*, Yolanda Moses, former president of The City University of New York and former president of the American Association of Higher Education, remarked, "I am very hopeful because so many Black women are in the pipeline and in leadership positions now" (Stewart, 2002, p. 25). Nevertheless, she acknowledged,

> There are still deep-held beliefs that keep Black women from being selected by boards (of trustees) and search committees. It's more subtle than it used to be, but it still exists on many campuses, Black and White. . . . We still have a long way to go. (p. 25)

The diplomas-to-doctorates pipeline is crucial, since there must be successors to African American women scholars and administrators who retire or leave the profession. We cannot overlook the point that the pipeline does not flow continuously on its own. There is a constant need for navigators who are familiar with the terrain and who can diminish and remove barriers. Mentors who have traversed the pipeline successfully can serve as navigators, guides, and advocates for African American women who come after them. Cheerleading by supporters on the home front, anchored in faith and a strong sense of purpose, is an ongoing source of inspiration and rejuvenation as African American women continue to rise.

Note

1. Comparatively, from 1994 to 2004 higher education enrollments for all students rose 21% to 17.3 million students (Cook & Cordova, 2007, p. 2). While the gains made by African American women were helpful toward closing college enrollment gaps with their European American peers, increases in college enrollments among African American men were comparatively sluggish. As such, the overall racial gap in college enrollments remains.

References

American Association of Community Colleges (AACC). (2006). *Community college president career and lifetime survey*. Washington, DC: Author.

American Council on Education (ACE). (2007). *The American college president: 2007 edition*. Washington, DC: Author.

Anderson, J. D. (1988). *The education of Blacks in the south*, 1860–1935. Chapel Hill, NC: University of North Carolina Press.

Bauman, R. M. (2002). A history of recording Black students at Oberlin College and the story of the missing record. Retrieved May 23, 2008, from http://www.oberlin.edu/archive/holdings/finding/RG5/SG4/S3/2002intro.html

Benjamin, L. (1997). *Black women in the academy: Promises and perils.* Gainesville, FL: University of Florida Press.

Berry, T. R., & Mizzelle, N. (2006). *From oppression to grace: Women of color and their dilemmas within the academy.* Sterling, VA: Stylus.

Cole, J. B., & Guy-Sheftall, B. (2003). *Gender talk: The struggle for women's equality in African American communities.* New York: Ballantine.

Cook, B. J., & Cordova, D. I. (2007). *Minorities in higher education: Twenty-second annual status report, 2007 supplement.* Washington, DC: American Council on Education.

DuBois, W. E. B. (1900). *The college-bred Negro. Report of a social study made under the direction of Atlanta University.* Proceedings of the fifth conference for The Study of the Negro Problems, Atlanta University, Atlanta, GA, May 29–30.

Ferguson, A. A. (2001). *Bad boys: Public schools in the making of Black masculinity.* Ann Arbor, MI: University of Michigan Press.

Giddings, P. (1984/2006). *When and where I enter: The impact of Black women on race and sex in America.* New York: William Morrow.

Haniff, N. Z. (1991). Epilogue. In W. R Allen, E. G. Epps, & N. Z. Haniff (Eds.), *College in Black and White: African American students in predominantly White and in historically Black public universities* (pp. 247–256). Albany, NY: State University of New York Press.

hooks, b. (1990). *Yearning: Race, gender and cultural politics.* Boston, MA: South End Press.

Hull, G. T., Bell Scott, P., & Smith, B. (1982). *All the women are White, all the Blacks are men, but some of us are brave: Black women's studies.* New York: The Feminist Press.

Mabokela, R., & Green, A. L. (Eds.). (2001). *Sisters of the academy: Emergent Black women scholars in the academy.* Sterling, VA: Stylus.

Matthews, W., & Jackson, K. W. (1991). Determinants of success for Black males and females in graduate and professional schools. In W. R Allen, E. G. Epps, & N. Z. Haniff (Eds.), *College in Black and White: African American students in predominantly White and in historically Black public universities* (pp. 197–208). Albany, NY: State University of New York Press.

National Center for Education Statistics (NCES). (2003). *Total fall enrollment in degree-granting institutions, by race/ethnicity of student and type and control of institution: Selected years, 1976 through 2001.* Retrieved August 21, 2007, from http://nces.ed.gov/programs/digest/d03/tables/dt209.asp

National Center for Education Statistics (NCES). (2007). *Total fall enrollment in degree-granting institutions, by race/ethnicity of student and type and control of institution: Selected years, 1976 through 2005.* Retrieved August 21, 2007, from http://nces.ed.gov/programs/digest/d07/tables/dt07_217.asp

Perkins, L. (1983). The impact of the "Cult of True Womanhood" on the education of Black women. *Journal of Social Issues, 39*(3), 17–28.

Renfro, G. H. (1993). *Life and works of Phillis Wheatley.* Salem: Ayer Company Publishers.

Schmidt, P. (2008, September 13). Many Black women veer off path to tenure, researchers say. *The Chronicle of Higher Education.* Retrieved September 13, 2008, from http://chronicle.com/news/article/5111/many-black-women-veer-off-path-to-tenure-researchers-say

Stewart, P. (2002, March 28). Responding to the voice of Black women [Electronic version]. *Black Issues in Higher Education, 19*(23), 25.

U.S. Department of Education, National Center for Education Statistics (NCES). (2003). *Digest of education statistics, Table 209.* Washington, DC: Author.

U.S. Department of Education, National Center for Education Statistics (NCES). (2007). *Digest of education statistics, Table 217.* Washington, DC: Author.

Vaughan, G. B., & Weisman, I. M. (1998). *The community college presidency at the millennium.* Washington, DC: Community College Press.

PART ONE

THE PRE-COLLEGIATE AND TRANSITIONAL EXPERIENCE

COLLEGE PREDISPOSITION AND THE DILEMMA OF BEING BLACK AND FEMALE IN HIGH SCHOOL

Adrienne D. Dixson and Crystal Renée Chambers

In *All the Women Are White, All the Blacks Are Men, But Some of Us Are Brave: Black Women's Studies* (1982), Hull, Bell Scott, and Smith put forth a case for Black women's atudies on the basis that the confluence of race, class, and gender exacts nonlinear tolls on the societal successes of African American women. This is no more the case in any setting than it is in education. While popular and academic literature pays much attention to the educational achievement of African American males, comparatively little of it explores factors contributing to the successes and failures of young Black women. Few works, of which Akom (2003) and Evans-Winters (2005) are exemplars, focus specifically on the academic successes of African American young women.

In this chapter we explore factors often considered predictors of college predisposition (Hossler & Gallagher, 1987) for young Black female high school students to gain an understanding of young Black women in high school and their views on the totality of their educational experience. In this vein, this chapter attempts to address and respond to the tendency to triage "all" Black students' educational experiences at the expense of Black women. Many have bought into the myth premised on Black women's greater success than that of their Black male counterparts based on several educational and employment indicators. The corollary is that researchers, policy makers, and educators need to focus on alleviating the plight of Black males. A core fallacy within this mythological construct is the glass ceiling effect. It is true that a larger proportion of Black women have educational and entry-level employment successes. Yet, Black women are not admitted into circles of power—although Black men, such as Vernon Jordan, Jesse Jackson, and, most recently, Barak Obama, have entry passes. In fact, a recent op-ed by Gloria Steinem highlights Black women's suppression by considering Obama's campaign had he been born female:

> The woman in question became a lawyer after some years as a community organizer. . . . Herself the daughter of a white American mother and a black African father—in this race-conscious country, she is considered black. . . . Be honest: Do you think this is the biography of someone who could be elected to the United States Senate? After less than one term there, do you believe she could be a viable candidate to head the most powerful nation on earth? (Steinem, 2008, ¶ 1)

It is important to note that, while we find Steinem's argument to be compelling with respect to the vexing ways that race and gender limit the opportunities for Black women, we recognize that Black males may have particular challenges in schooling that contribute to undereducation or lower rates of achievement than those of Black females. We also argue that Black females do in fact have challenges and experiences of a different sort, ones with a history that places them in a precarious position with respect to the politics of race and gender, as the response to Steinem's op-ed piece demonstrates.[1] Further, we posit that these differences may contribute to educational experiences that over time hamper social relations, especially with Black men (Cole & Guy-Sheftall, 2003). Thus, in this chapter, we address the tendency to essentialize (assume that all Black women are the same), the experiences of Black women. Engaging in this line of inquiry will enrich our knowledge of both positive and negative influences contributing to Black women's academic success generally, college predisposition, and eventual college enrollment.

Theoretical Framework

Analysis in this work is evaluated from the view of critical race feminism. Critical race feminism encourages an analysis of racial phenomena that goes beyond the essentialism underlying purely race or gendered perspectives on social phenomena (Wing, 2003). Critical race feminism is a derivative of critical race theory (CRT) and Black feminist theory, containing aspects of both. CRT scholars, as captured by Matsuda, Lawrence, Delgado, & Crenshaw (1993), identify six themes that define CRT:

1. Critical race theory recognizes that racism is endemic to American life.
2. Critical race theory expresses skepticism toward dominant legal claims of neutrality, objectivity, colorblindness, and meritocracy.
3. Critical race theory challenges a historicism and insists on a contextual/historical analysis of the law. . . . Critical race theorists . . . adopt a stance that presumes that racism has contributed to all contemporary manifestations of group advantage and disadvantage.
4. Critical race theory insists on recognition of the experiential knowledge of people of color and our communities of origin in analyzing law and society.
5. Critical race theory is interdisciplinary.
6. Critical race theory works toward the end of eliminating racial oppression as part of the broader goal of ending all forms of oppression (p. 6).

Similarly acknowledging the endemic status of sexism and classism in society, radical feminist Catherine MacKinnon (1991) identified the argument underlying feminist theory, that by dividing society on the basis of sex, "social relations of gender are created, expressed, and directed" for purposes of maintaining male dominance in both the public and private sphere (p. 1). However, feminist traditions are riddled by racial fractures as White feminist scholars historically have expropriated the experiences of women of color on an as-needed basis, while discarding racialized perspectives when inconvenient (Collins, 1990/2000; Giddings, 1984).

Critical race feminism (CRF) interlays the two perspectives as academic gender discussions centering on the experience of middle-class White women and discussions of race on the plight of Black men (Wing, 2003). For example, when considering work on the crime of rape, Black feminist scholarship argued that focusing on the bodily integrity of women largely ignored the tolls of criminality/perceived criminality in African American communities.

Neither set of works addressed one important intersection, social perceptions of the inability of women of color to be raped,[2] with resultant disparities in reporting and sentencing.

A fundamental aspect of CRF scholarship is the notion that women of color face discrimination on multiple, often interlocking/intersecting levels that include, but are not limited to, gender, race and class. Thus, the experiences for women of color go beyond the idea that they are simply persons of color plus gender, or White women plus skin tone, but that these issues of intersectionality speak to the ways in which White male patriarchy and racial oppression (and some would argue heterosexism and ableism) work against women of color (Wing, 2003). Similar to Deborah King's (1995) multiple jeopardy thesis, Wing suggests in her article, "Brief Reflections toward a Multiplicative Theory and Praxis of Being," that,

> We, as black women, can no longer afford to think of ourselves or let the law think of us as merely the sum of separate parts that can be added together or subtracted from, until a white male or female stands before you. The actuality of our layered experience is *multiplicative* [emphasis in the original]. Multiply each of my parts together, 1x1x1x1x1, and you have one indivisible being. If you divide one of these parts from one you still have *one* [emphasis in the original]. (p. 31)

When conducting research, failure to consider race, class, and gender dynamics overlooks the complexity of young Black women's experiences. When considering the context of high school, is it the case that all Black girls are "ghetto" or "loud" (Fordham, 1993; Lei, 2003)? Or are there variances in experiences along class lines, geographical lines, or even religious lines?[3]

In the study at hand, critical race feminism is insightful as it helps to explain differences in college predisposition between young Black women and other students (Gafford Muhammad, 2006a; Freeman, 2005). College predisposition (Hossler & Gallagher, 1987) or predetermination (Freeman, 2005) denotes the time at which a student begins an active college search, taking concrete steps toward college enrollment. In the higher education literature, the disparity between the educational aspirations of young African Americans and college predisposition is documented and is significant (e.g., Hamrick & Stage, 2004; Kim, 2004; Plank & Jordan, 2001; Somers, Cofer, & VanderPutten, 2002; Teranishi, Ceja, Antonio, Allen, & McDonough, 2004; Thomas, 2004). However, few works disaggregate predisposition on the basis of gender (Galotti & Mark, 1994; Hamrick & Stage, 1998), and no works do that examine the intersections of race and gender. Using a critical race feminist frame, we seek to fill this gap in the literature.

Data Source

This study uses restricted data from the base year and first follow-up to the 2002 Education Longitudinal Study (ELS 02/04). The ELS 02/04 survey includes data for a nationally representative sample of 21,757 students who were 10th-graders in 2002, the base year of the study. Of this base year sample, 2,074 students are Black. In the first follow-up, most students are high school seniors. In the National Educational Longitudinal Survey of 1988, the predecessor to the ELS, 62% of African American women enrolled in college, compared to only 53% of young Black men (Gafford Muhammad, 2006b). It is expected that in the more recent ELS, the relative difference in college enrollment between young Black men and Black women will have declined, albeit slightly, as per enrollment gains made by young Black men ("Say What," 2006). College enrollment rates among young Black women have increased as well. The present study explores factors contributing to their success compared to the population more broadly, as racial explanations fail to explain the present enrollment gap between young Blacks, and differences in enrollments between young Black and White women are small (King, 2000).

Methodology

We use descriptive analysis to explore factors known to influence college predisposition, including background (student socioeconomic status and school urbanicity as well as size); student's academic status (program of study, grade level, and dropout status); academic achievement and proficiency (combined and mathematics standardized examination scores as well as measures of mathematics proficiency); parental involvement and support; teacher expectations; student involvement in school; and peer influences. In addition, we explore factors of the student's assessment of the learning environment, whether young Black women perceive the academic environment to be just and fair. These factors include student self-report of disciplinary action and the appearance of fairness in the exercise of discipline with others. Finally, college predisposition is measured by student responses to the question of their plans after high school. Most variables are measured in the base year, which is the sophomore year for students in this cohort. The departure from this generality is the factor of college predisposition, which is measured 2 years after the base year, the 12th grade for the majority of the sample. Along with general descriptive statistics, we use chi-square analyses to compare individual and school factors contributing to student success between young Black women and the rest of the ELS sample.

Results

Background

Young Black women come from socioeconomic backgrounds that are less wealthy than the average student and are clustered toward the bottom half of the socioeconomic distribution (Mean SES_{BW} = -0.21, SD = 0.67; Mean $SES_{All\ Other}$ = 0.1, SD = 0.74; t = 13.56, p = 0.0001). Young Black women are more likely to matriculate in urban public high schools, although their numbers in suburban high schools are sizable. Differences in school size, urbanicity, and control were assessed using chi-square analyses comparing young Black women to the rest of the ELS population. For this section, 106 women legitimately skipped answers to these items. Of the 946 women in this sample, 452 were enrolled in urban high schools, 388 in suburban high schools, and 106 in rural schools (χ^2 School Urbanicity = 1,827.31, df = 2, p = 0.0001). Only 10% of the young women attended schools with enrollments over 2,000 students (χ^2 School Enrollment = 1,148.91, df = 9, p = 0.0001), and nearly 87% attended public schools (χ^2 School Control = 11,278.29, df = 2, p = 0.0001). While significant, these differences are not practically large, meaning it is not uncommon to have high school enrollments of 2,000 students, as the grouping of other students encompasses other students of color concentrated at the schools in which young Black women matriculate.

Young Black women progress through high school at rates comparable to their age-group counterparts regardless of race. According to self-reported data, young Black women are only slightly less likely than their age-group peers to be enrolled in college preparatory tracks, although they are enrolled in vocational tracks disproportionately. Together these factors suggest that young Black women have a sense of focus when considering their high school curriculum. In terms of their rate of progress through high school, differences in being on grade level and dropping out are slight, less than 2%, although statistically significant (see Table 1.1 for Frequencies; χ^2 HS Program = 24812.455, *df* = 7, *p* = 0.0001; χ^2 Grade Level = 92188.440, *df* = 8, *p* = 0.0001; χ^2 Dropout = 12159.976, *df* = 1, *p* = 0.0001).

Academic Achievement

We measured academic achievement using composite math and reading exam scores in grade 10. Given the strong predictive power of mathematics in college enrollment (Adelman, 2006), to understand propensity toward college enrollment, we were particularly concerned about the math performance of young Black women. Results are detailed in Table 1.2. Differences between test score means are strong and are standard across composite and mathematics scores. African Americans generally do not perform as well on standardized exams, and women on average do not perform as well in mathematics. One key factor in considering the performance of young Black

TABLE 1.1
Frequencies, Program of Study, Grade Level, and Dropout

	Black Women (N = 946)		Peers (N = 13,310)	
	N	%*	N	%*
Program of Study				
General	239	25.26	3,941	19.61
College Prep	461	28.73	6,793	51.04
Vocational	112	11.83	1,056	7.93
Grade Level in 2002**				
Missing	81	8.56	582	4.37
10th	2	0.21	20	0.15
11th	18	1.9	155	1.16
12th	864	91.33	12,479	93.76
Ungraded Program	8	0.84	74	0.23
Ever Dropped Out				
No	919	97.14	13,016	97.79
Yes	27	2.9	294	2.2

* Combined percentages do not necessarily total 100% due to rounding error.
** "On time" status is at the 12th grade level.

TABLE 1.2
Standardized Exam Scores, Means, and Standard Deviations

	Black Women (N = 946)	Peers (N = 13,310)
Composite Reading & Math Scores	44.03*	50.83*
	(11.18)	(12.39)
Math Score	43.33*	50.91*
	(11.12)	(12.38)

*$p \leq 0.0001$.

women is stereotype threat (Steele & Aronson, 2000). Here, race and gender may conflate to act as a double bind. Actual performance, however, does not hamper expectations for future performance whether these expectations are from parents or teachers, as discussed in the following section.

Parental Involvement and Support

While the percentage difference is small, young Black women are more likely to report that their parents are often engaged in their high school educational careers. These differences are statistically significant (see Table 1.3 for frequencies; e.g., χ^2 Check Homework $= 548.461$, $df = 7$, $p = 0.0001$; χ^2 Help with Homework $= 312.505$, $df = 6$, $p = 0.0001$; $\chi^2 = 505.886$, $df = 7$, $p = 0.0001$). In addition, young Black women are more likely to report high parental expectations regarding success at school (see Table 1.4 for frequencies; χ^2 Parent Expectations $= 2508.934$, $df = 8$, $p = 0.0001$), and parents are more likely to want to send them to college (e.g., χ^2 Mother's Desire $= 4853.279$, $df = 10$ $p = 0.0001$) and have them persist through a graduate degree.

School/Teacher Dynamics

Young Black women are more likely to feel supported by their teachers than other students in their age group and are more likely to perceive that their teachers expect success from them (χ^2 Teacher Expectations $= 1306.264$, $df = 8$, $p = 0.0001$) (see Table 1.5). While only slightly more likely to believe that their favorite teacher wants them to go to college, they are less likely, by 3 percentage points, to view their favorite teacher as not caring about their

TABLE 1.3
Frequencies, Parental Involvement

	Black Women (N = 946)		Peers (N = 13,310)	
	N	%*	N	%*
How Often Parents Check Homework				
Missing	231	24.0	2,500	19.0
Never	86	09.0	1,570	12.0
Rarely	138	15.0	2,280	17.0
Sometimes	221	23.0	3,127	23.0
Often	270	29.0	3,833	29.0
How Often Parents Help With Homework				
Missing	223	24.0	2,467	19.0
Never	121	13.0	1,927	14.0
Rarely	202	21.0	3,260	24.0
Sometimes	262	28.0	4,208	32.0
Often	138	15.0	1,448	11.0
Special Privileges Given for Good Grades				
Missing	237	25.0	2,591	19.0
Never	71	08.0	1,542	12.0
Rarely	103	11.0	1,970	15.0
Sometimes	213	23.0	3,767	28.0
Often	322	34.0	3,440	26.0
How Often Discussed School Courses With Parents				
Missing	253	27.0	2,834	21.0
Never	120	13.0	1,834	14.0
Sometimes	329	35.0	5,540	42.0
Often	244	26.0	3,102	23.0
How Often Discussed Grades With Parents				
Missing	253	27.0	2,885	22.0
Never	45	05.0	683	05.0
Sometimes	243	26.0	4,513	34.0
Often	405	43.0	5,229	39.0

* Combined percentages do not necessarily total 100% due to rounding error.

postsecondary education careers. However, their favorite teacher aside, young Black women seem slightly less enthused regarding the campus climate, although the general view is positive and tracks patterns among other students. In this regard young Black women perceive that students get along well with teachers and that teachers praise students' efforts, just not as

TABLE 1.4
Student Perceptions of Parental Aspirations

| | Black Women (N = 946) | | | | Peers (N = 13,310) | | | |
| | Grade 10 | | Grade 12 | | Grade 10 | | Grade 12 | |
	N	%*	N	%*	N	%*	N	%*
Parents Expect Success in School								
Missing	111	12.0	n/a	—	1,360	10.0	n/a	—
Strongly Agree	542	57.0	n/a	—	6,417	48.0	n/a	—
Agree	254	27.0	n/a	—	4,816	36.0	n/a	—
Disagree	32	03.0	n/a	—	555	4.0	n/a	—
Strongly Disagree	7	01.0	n/a	—	162	1.0	n/a	—
How Far in School Mother Wants Child to Go								
Missing	249	26.0	22	2.0	2,535	19.0	438	3.0
Less Than High School	14	1.0	24	3.0	206	2.0	192	1.0
High School Graduation/GED	36	4.0	63	7.0	525	4.0	736	6.0
Attend/Complete a Two-Year Institution	41	4.0	61	6.0	428	3.0	1131	8.0
Attend a Four-Year College	34	4.0	42	4.0	327	2.0	409	3.0
College Graduate	214	23.0	240	25.0	4546	34.0	4,952	37.0
Obtain a Graduate or Advanced Degree	343	36.0	430	45.0	4145	31.0	4,574	34.0
Don't Know	50	5.0	64	7.0	598	4.0	878	7.0
Obtain a Graduate or Advanced Degree	271	29.0	336	36.0	3929	30.0	4,409	33.0
Don't Know	92	10.0	147	16.0	5820	44.0	1,173	9.0
Father's Desire for Child After High School								
Missing	n/a	—	185	20.0	n/a	—	1,419	11.0
College	n/a	—	558	59.0	n/a	—	8,672	65.0
Work	n/a	—	21	2.0	n/a	—	,,,581	4.0
Trade School/Apprenticeship	n/a	—	9	1.0	n/a	—	,,,252	2.0
Military	n/a	—	18	2.0	n/a	—	,,,238	2.0
Father's Desire for Child After High School								
Marriage	n/a	—	6	1.0	n/a	—	25	0.0
"They think I should do what I want."	n/a	—	51	5.0	n/a	—	1,516	11.0
"They don't care."	n/a	—	98	1.0	n/a	—	,,,607	5.0

* Combined percentages do not necessarily total 100% due to rounding error.

TABLE 1.5
Student Perceptions of Teacher Expectations and Aspirations

	Black Women (N = 946)		Peers (N = 13,310)	
	N	%*	N	%*
Teachers Expect Success in School				
Missing	118	12.0	1,386	10.0
Strongly Agree	188	20.0	1,704	13.0
Agree	390	41.0	5,607	42.0
Disagree	209	22.0	3,805	29.0
Strongly Disagree	41	4.0	808	6.0
Favorite Teacher's Desire for Respondent After High School				
Missing	42	4.0	3,703	28.0
College	518	55.0	7,144	54.0
Work	2	0.0	80	1.0
Trade School/Apprenticeship	6	1.0	137	1.0
Military	3	0.0	66	0.0
Marriage	3	0.0	15	0.0
"They think I should do what I want."	32	3.0	825	6.0
"They don't care."	40	4.0	940	7.0

* Combined percentages do not necessarily total 100% due to rounding error.

strongly as their peers. Young Black women are equally as likely as their peers to assess their school environment as spirited.

One key difference is in the perception of misbehaving students. Young Black women perceive that misbehaving students disrupt class and disturb the learning environment, by a factor of 10%. See Table 1.6. They are slightly more likely to believe that everyone knows what the rules are, by a factor of 4%, but are 9% less likely to perceive the rules are fair. However their overall assessment of the application of rules square well with their peers. Fifty-two percent of the women believed that punishments were the same no matter who you were as compared to 56% of their peers. See Table 1.7. Perhaps rather than being revolted by disciplinary actions against young Black men, young Black women have internalized school discourses on appropriate behavior to view young Black men as deviant "others," so they buy into the system of penalties. Regarding their own disciplinary record, young Black women are more likely to report an uncheckered history; yet, they are more likely to perceive the disciplinary system as unfair, albeit only slightly (see

TABLE 1.6
Student Assessment of the School Environment

	Black Women (N = 946)		Peers (N = 13,310)	
	N	%*	N	%*
Students Get Along Well With Teachers				
Missing	88	9.0	1,322	10.0
Strongly Agree	41	4.0	817	6.0
Agree	442	47.0	8,626	65.0
Disagree	308	33.0	2,273	17.0
Strongly Disagree	47	5.0	272	2.0
There Is Real School Spirit				
Missing	89	9.0	1,373	10.0
Strongly Agree	129	14.0	2,162	16.0
Agree	422	45.0	6,430	48.0
Disagree	229	24.0	2,794	21.0
Strongly Disagree	57	6.0	550	4.0
Teachers Are Interested in Students				
Missing	106	11.0	1,513	11.0
Strongly Agree	101	11.0	1,861	14.0
Agree	489	52.0	7,321	55.0
Disagree	189	20.0	2,258	17.0
Strongly Disagree	41	4.0	357	3.0
Teachers Praise Effort				
Missing	94	10.0	1,415	11.0
Strongly Agree	141	15.0	1,813	14.0
Agree	413	44.0	6,027	45.0
Disagree	236	25.0	3,605	27.0
Strongly Disagree	42	4.0	450	3.0
In Class Often Feels Put Down by Teachers				
Missing	93	10.0	1,374	10.0
Strongly Agree	19	2.0	279	2.0
Agree	85	9.0	1,183	9.0
Disagree	441	47.0	7,004	53.0
Strongly Disagree	288	30.0	3,470	26.0
Disruptions Get in the Way of Learning				
Missing	91	10.0	1,397	10.0
Strongly Agree	152	16.0	1,221	9.0
Agree	314	33.0	3,954	30.0
Disagree	277	29.0	5,387	40.0
Strongly Disagree	92	10.0	1,351	10.0

* Combined percentages do not necessarily total 100% due to rounding error.

TABLE 1.7
Student Perceptions of Justice at School

	Black Women (N = 946)		Peers (N = 13,310)	
	N	%*	N	%*
Everyone Knows What School Rules Are				
Missing	104	11.0	1,334	10.0
Strongly Agree	269	28.0	7,583	57.0
Agree	447	47.0	1,844	14.0
Disagree	107	11.0	249	2.0
Strongly Disagree	19	2.0	2,300	17.0
School Rules Are Fair				
Missing	107	11.0	1,459	11.0
Strongly Agree	57	6.0	817	6.0
Agree	292	31.0	5,937	45.0
Disagree	347	37.0	3,947	30.0
Strongly Disagree	133	14.0	1,150	9.0
Punishment Same No Matter Who You Are				
Missing	112	12.0	1,423	11.0
Strongly Agree	168	18.0	1,993	15.0
Agree	323	34.0	5,476	41.0
Disagree	242	26.0	3,085	23.0
Strongly Disagree	101	11.0	1,333	10.0

* Combined percentages do not necessarily total 100% due to rounding error.

Table 1.7). Qualitative data analysis would give a richer understanding of these contradictory feelings and a better understanding of relations between young Black men and women in high school.

Peer Influences

Previous work using NELS: 88/00 (Gafford Muhammad, 2006b) suggests that the influence of peer effects on the college enrollment of young Black women is not significant; therefore, while peer effects are viable in the general population, the expectation within this subpopulation is that there should be no significant influence/predictive capacity with respect to college predisposition. It does seem to be the case that young Black women choose friends who are similarly academically oriented and are more likely than others to attend classes regularly, study, and get good grades. Young Black

TABLE 1.8
Student Perceptions of Friends' Valuation of Education

	Black Women (N = 946)		Peers (N = 13,310)	
	N	%*	N	%*
Important to Friends to Attend Classes Regularly				
Missing	396	42.0	4,401	33.0
Not Important	13	1.0	378	3.0
Somewhat Important	200	21.0	3,732	28.0
Very Important	337	36.0	4,799	36.0
Important to Friends to Study				
Missing	380	40.0	4,351	33.0
Not Important	36	4.0	895	7.0
Somewhat Important	249	26.0	4,945	37.0
Very Important	281	30.0	3,119	23.0

* Combined percentages do not necessarily total 100% due to rounding error.

women are as likely as their peers to report that friends see college as important, but find college completion less so. See Table 1.8.

College Predisposition

When not controlling for environmental and background factors, young Black women in the aggregate are less likely than their peers two years after 10th grade to have concrete college plans, respectively 71% as compared to

TABLE 1.9
College Predisposition

	Black Women (N = 946)		Peers (N = 13,310)	
	N	%*	N	%*
Plans to Continue Education After High School (F1)				
Missing	130	14.0	2,148	16.0
No, don't plan to continue	673	71.0	8,819	66.0
Yes, right after high school	106	11.0	1,479	11.0
Yes, after out of high school 1 year	6	1.0	196	1.0
Yes, after out of high school over 1 year	30	3.0	849	6.0
Don't know	1	0.0	49	0.0

*Combined percentages do not necessarily total 100% due to rounding error.

66%. See Table 1.9. This confirms Freeman's (2005) finding that young Blacks generally are delayed in the college choice process. Often due to informational constraints and limited social networking experiences with successful college graduates, young Black students have a comparative disadvantage in gathering information on how to position themselves and apply to college. This process is impeded further by strains on school counselor duties in urban high schools. Such strains include: disproportionate student-to-counselor ratio, administrative duties unrelated to traditional conceptions of school counseling, and health and welfare matters. Thus, college preparation becomes a luxury task for high school counselors, particularly in under-resourced urban districts (Adelman, 2002; Fitch & Marshall, 2004).

The resiliency of young Black women is found in their comparable rates of college predisposition by grade ten. They report being predisposed to enter college within one year of completing high school and are at parity with their peers, 11% directly after graduation and another 1% a year thereafter. Young Black women are 3% less likely to respond that they will go to college two or more years after high school graduation.

Conclusion

The findings from this study suggest that young Black women value higher education and believe they have the support to pursue a college education. While they report generally positive perceptions about school with respect to school climate, the quality of teaching, and relationships with peers, they are aware of shortcomings of school disciplinary systems, although they do seem to agree that disciplinary measures in school are important for an effective learning environment.

This initial examination of the ELS is cursory, an aggregation of young Black girls sampled. We suggest, therefore, that microanalyses at the school and classroom level and using qualitative methods might explain the complexities of their schooling experiences and the seeming contradictions in the data. These contradictions suggest that conditions within schools, albeit not directed at young Black women, may impinge on the integrity of learning for young Black women and the rigor with which they pursue education. Thus, even though young Black women do not bear the brunt of many injustices in the classroom, they are witnesses to the classroom management strategies of their teachers and unfairness in the dispensing of disciplinary authority (Lewis, 2003). The effects may not show up in the form of lower academic performance; however, the psychological integrity of young Black women and their interactions with their peers, non-Black as well as males, is at stake.

Notes

1. Princeton University political science professor Melissa Harris Lacewell has taken Steinem to task for her op-ed article. Lacewell points out that Steinem's critique of Obama essentially places Black women in the middle of the argument between Obama and Hillary Clinton, as has been a historical tactic of first- and second-wave White feminists. For more on this discussion see, http://www.demo cracynow.org/2008/1/14/race and gender in presidential politics.

2. It is important to note that CRT scholar Kimberlé Crenshaw argues that much of rape research presumes a White female victim (Crenshaw, 1995).

3. Another important line of inquiry with respect to the educational aspirations and experiences of Black females is to examine more closely the impact of social class and social geography. That is, some researchers are beginning to look at the suburbanization of the Black middle class (Adelman, 2006; Feagin & Sikes, 1994; Lacy, 2002, 2004; Patillo-McCoy, 1999). We would argue that Black middle class girls face a different set of challenges due in part to the racial isolation they may experience from being educated in predominantly White suburban areas (Lewis, 2003).

References

Adelman, C. (2006). *The toolbox revisited: Paths to degree completion from high school through college.* Washington DC: U.S. Department of Education.

Adelman, H. S. (2002). School counselor and school reform: New directions. *Professional School Counseling, 5,* 261–268.

Akom, A. A. (2003). Reexamining resistance as oppositional behavior: The Nation of Islam and the creation of a Black achievement ideology. *Sociology of Education, 76*(4), 305–325.

Cole, J. B., & Guy-Sheftall, B. (2003). *Gender talk: The struggle for women's equality in African American communities.* New York: Ballantine.

Collins, P. H. (1990/2000). *Black feminist thought: Knowledge, consciousness, and the politics of empowerment.* New York: Routledge.

Crenshaw, K. (1995). Mapping the margins: Intersectionality, identity politics, and violence against women of color. In K. Crenshaw, N. Gotanda, G. Peller, & K. Thomas (Eds.), *Critical Race Theory: The Key Writings That Formed the Movement* (pp. 357–383). New York: The New Press.

Evans-Winters, V. E. (2005). *Teaching Black girls: Resiliency in urban classrooms.* New York: Peter Lang.

Feagin, J., & Sikes, M. (1994). *Living with racism: The Black middle class experience.* Boston, MA: Beacon Press.

Fitch, T. J., & Marshall, J. L. (2004). What counselors do in high-achieving schools: A study on the role of the school counselor. *Professional School Counseling, 7,* 172–177.

Fordham, S. (1993). "Those loud Black girls": (Black) women, silence, and gender "passing" in the academy. *Anthropology and Education Quarterly 24*(1), 3–32.

Freeman, K. (2005). *African Americans and college choice: The influence of family and school.* Albany, NY: State University of New York Press.

Gafford Muhammad, C. (2006a). [Review of the book *African Americans and college choice: The influence of family and school*]. *The Review of Higher Education, 29*(2), 247–248.

Gafford Muhammad, C. (2006b). *Gender differences in African American college enrollment: The role of extracurricular participation.* Unpublished manuscript.

Galotti, K. M., & Mark, M. C. (1994). How do high-school students structure an important life decision—A short-term longitudinal study of the college decision-making process. *Research in Higher Education, 35*(5), 589–607.

Giddings, P. (1984). *When and where I enter: The impact of Black women on race and sex in America.* New York: William Morrow.

Hamrick, F. A., & Stage, F. K. (1998). High minority enrollment, high school-lunch rates: Predisposition to college. *Review of Higher Education, 21*(4), 343–357.

Hamrick, F. A., & Stage, F. K. (2004). College predisposition at high-minority enrollment, low-income schools. *Review of Higher Education, 27*(2), 151–168.

Hossler, D., & Gallagher, K. S. (1987). Studying student choice—A 3-phase model and the implications for policy-makers. *College & University, 62*(3), 207–221.

Hull, G. T., Bell Scott, P., & Smith, B. (Eds.) (1982). *All the women are White, all the Blacks are men, but some of us are brave: Black women's studies.* New York: The Feminist Press.

Kim, D. (2004). The effect of financial aid on students' college choice: Differences by racial groups. *Research in Higher Education, 45*(1), 43–70.

King, D. K. (1995). Multiple jeopardy, multiple consciousness: The context of a Black feminist ideology. In B. Guy-Sheftall (Ed.), *Words of fire: An anthology of African-American feminist thought* (pp. 294–318). New York: The New Press.

King, J. E. (2000). *Gender equity in higher education: Are male students at a disadvantage?* Washington, DC: American Council on Education Center for Policy Analysis.

Lacy, K. R. (2002). A part of the neighborhood? Negotiating race in American suburbs. *International Journal of Sociology and Social Policy, 22*(1), 39–74.

Lacy, K. R. (2004). Black spaces, black places: Strategic assimilation and identity construction in middle-class suburbia. *Ethnic and Racial Studies, 27*(6), 908–930.

Lei, J. L. (2003). (Un)Necessary Toughness?: "Those loud Black girls and those quiet Asian boys." *Anthropology and Education Quarterly, 34*(2), 158–181.

Lewis, A. E. (2003). *Race in the schoolyard: Negotiating the color line in classrooms and communities*. New Brunswick, NJ: Rutgers University Press.

MacKinnon, C. (1991). *Toward a feminist theory of the state*. Cambridge, MA: Harvard University Press.

Matsuda, M. J., Lawrence, C. R., Delgado, R., & Crenshaw, K.W. (Eds.). (1993). *Words that wound: Critical race theory, assaultive speech, and the First Amendment*. Boulder, CO: Westview Press.

Patillo-McCoy, M. (1999). *Black picket fences: Privilege and peril among the Black middle class*. Chicago, IL: University of Chicago Press.

Plank, S. B., & Jordan, W. J. (2001). Effects of information, guidance, and actions on postsecondary destinations: A study of talent loss. *American Educational Research Journal, 38*(4), 947–979.

Say what? Black men are actually making progress in college enrollments. (2006, July 6). *Journal of Blacks in Higher Education*. Retrieved July 27, 2003, from http://www.jbhe.com/latest/index070606.html

Somers, P., Cofer, J., & VanderPutten, J. (2002). The early bird goes to college: The link between early college aspirations and postsecondary matriculation. *Journal of College Student Development, 43*(1), 93–107.

Steele, C. M., & Aronson, J. (2000). Stereotype threat and the intellectual test performance of African Americans. *Stereotypes and prejudice: Essential readings* (pp. 369–389). New York: Psychology Press.

Steinem, G. (2008). Women are never front-runners. *The New York Times*. Retrieved January 24, 2008 from http://www.nytimes.com/2008/01/08/opinion/08steinem .html?_r=1&em&ex=1200114000&en=f7ff1506bb86d225&ei=5087%0A&o ref=slogin

Teranishi, R. T., Ceja, M., Antonio, A. L., Allen, R. A., & McDonough, P. M. (2004). The college-choice process for Asian Pacific Americans: Ethnicity and socioeconomic class in context. *The Review of Higher Education, 27*(4), 527–551.

Thomas, K. M. (2004). Where college-bound students send their SAT scores: Does race matter? *Social Science Quarterly, 85*(5), 1374–1389.

Wing, A. K. (2003). Brief reflections toward a multiplicative theory and praxis of being. In Adrien Wing (Ed.), *Critical race feminism: A reader*. New York: NYU Press.

2

"MAKING A DOLLAR OUT OF FIFTEEN CENTS"

The Early Educational Investments of Young Black Women

Crystal Renée Chambers

In a mid-20th-century article on American folk culture, researcher Lucy Nulton (1948) contextualizes the jump rope rhymes of American youth as children's perception and expression of the adult world. While the rhymes were often loaded with inappropriate adult content and stereotypes, they often included hidden messages. The first stanza of one such rhyme ends by pointing out a racially offensive character "sitting on the fence," who is trying to "make a dollar, out of fifteen cents" (Yoffie, 1947, p. 49). The underlying message here is that of frugality, a characteristic historically attributed rightly or wrongly to persons of Asian descent. Nulton (1948) does not discuss this rhyme as specific to young Black girls; yet, personal and anecdotal inquiry confirm that the line survives and continues to resonate in African American communities. As young Black girls jump to the beat of single ropes or double Dutch, there is an imbedded message to do the best with what you have: to make a dollar out of 15 cents.

This chapter uses data and statistics calculated from the National Educational Longitudinal Survey of 1988 (NELS:88/00) to analyze the early educational investments of Black girls: how high school students translate limited human, social, and cultural capital resources into educational attainment benchmarks, namely college (postsecondary) enrollment. We use the term college loosely to define all formal educational endeavors after high school.

This point of college enrollment along the educational attainment continuum is of particular importance to African Americans. The Black-White earnings gap continues at a pace that has held steady for more than 30 years: the overall median income of Blacks is 61% of that of Whites. Having some college raises the earnings median of Blacks to just over $20,000 annually. Yet, having a bachelor's degree boosts the median earnings of Blacks overall to 90% of those of Whites ("Higher Education Is the Major Force," 2007).[1]

Whether a young woman selects a four-year college or university, a two-year community or junior college, or a trade school postsecondary experience, the core of this analysis is that regardless of the circumstances into which they are born or the quality of schools they are slotted to attend, young Black women, on average, are making the most of it. By way of a road map, this chapter begins with an overview of contemporary college enrollment trends among young Black women placed within a context of human capital theory. General trends indicate that not only do young Black women outpace Black men, but often White men as well in college enrollment. The chapter then backtracks to the human, social, and cultural capital investments young Black women make during their high school years. For young Black women, previous academic achievement and investments in additional units of mathematics are significant contributors to their greater propensity to enroll in college. However, their greatest feat and most substantial advantage in the quest toward college enrollment is their failure to engage the negative trappings of socioeconomic circumstance.

College Enrollment Trends Among Young Black Women

According to data from the U.S. Census Bureau (2006), from 1990 to 2005, the college enrollment rate of all students, ages 18–24, rose nearly 7%, to 38.9%. These data are presented in Table 2.1. By 2005, nearly 50% of all high school graduates in this age bracket went to college. Among young Blacks, however, gains in college enrollment for 18- to 24-year-olds rose only 7%, to 32.7% of young Blacks. Only 40% of all Black high school graduates enrolled in college. By gender, college enrollments among young Black men increased a mere 1.8%, to 27.9% of Black 18- to 24-year-old males, and 35% of Black male high school graduates. Young Black women, however, made gains of 13.1% over this same period. By 2005, 37.1% of Black women ages

TABLE 2.1
Five-Year Interval Panel Data, U.S. College Student Enrollment, 1990–2005*

Gender Year	All Students			Black Students		
	Total Population of 18- to 24-year-olds (in thousands)	Percentage Enrolled in College	Percentage of High School Graduates Enrolled in College	Total Population of 18- to 24-year-olds (in thousands)	Percentage Enrolled in College	Percentage of High School Graduates Enrolled in College
All						
2005	27,855	38.9	49.3	3,964	32.7	40.0
2000	26,658	35.5	43.3	4,013	30.3	39.4
1995	24,900	34.3	42.4	3,625	27.3	35.4
1990	24,852	32.0	39.1	3,520	25.4	33.0
Male						
2005	14,077	35.3	43.2	1,897	27.9	35.0
2000	13,338	32.6	40.9	1,885	24.9	33.8
1995	12,351	33.1	41.8	1,660	25.9	34.4
1990	12,134	32.3	40.1	1,634	26.1	34.4
Female						
2005	13,778	42.5	55.8	2,067	37.1	44.9
2000	13,319	38.4	45.6	2,128	35.1	43.9
1995	12,548	35.5	43.1	1,965	28.4	36.2
1990	12,718	31.8	38.4	1,886	24.8	31.8

* Data from the October 2006 Current Population Survey, conducted by the U.S. Bureau of the Census.

18–24 were enrolled in college. Among young Black female high school grad-uates, this figure is 44.9%. Thus, the gains made in African American college enrollments are lopsided, largely attributable to the considerable gains of Black women.

The Interlocked Frames of Human, Social, and Cultural Capital Theory

Human capital theory provides a framework from the field of economics for understanding how people make choices about their education (Becker, 1993). Human capital theory can look at different points along the education-employment continuum and provide a framework estimating one's prob-ability of further education or earnings based on one's prior achieve-ments. The particular application of human capital in this study is college enrollment.

The logic used in human capital theory is the mind-set of an investor. One will invest in a particular product, let's say a stock, if it is affordable and the value of the stock is expected to exceed its initial cost. In the same vein, a student will consider the costs of enrolling in college: tuition and fees, for-gone earnings, opportunity costs, and time taken from other worthwhile activities such as home and family. The student will also consider his or her academic ability, reflecting on high school performance and the quality of interaction with faculty, classmates, and support personnel. Here the student is assessing whether he or she can do it—an "affordability" question aside from the financial ability to pay for an education—the ability to succeed at the endeavor. The student will then compare these costs to the potential benefits of a college education.

Human capital theory therefore assumes a singular rational actor, con-ducting a cost-benefit analysis and deciding for or against a college educa-tion. However, ask any parent his or her reflection on the assumption that most 18- to 24-year-olds are rational and you are likely to hear that this over-simplification is grossly inaccurate. Beyond a parental assessment of the rationality of young people, contextual elements do matter. To that extent, social and cultural capital theoretical frames potentially improve on the human capital model by including communal contacts and norms.

Social capital refers to social networks (Coleman, 1988; Schuller, Baron, & Field, 2000). Looking solely at social capital, one's expected return from education would not be based on "what you know," but rather "whom you know." The "people you know" are important for their positive, or negative, influences as well as their connectedness to educational processes. The ultimate direct connection for a prospective student may be the provost of a major institution and/or a degree of separation or two from an elected official. However, family members who have gone to college, teachers, guidance counselors and other support personnel, and community leaders with special emphasis on the church are key persons who often exert positive pressure in favor of college for African Americans. In addition, these persons often have the know-how to help students navigate college admissions processes and/or the social capital to connect students further to persons who can help.

In contrast to social capital's "whom you know," cultural capital refers to "what you know." More specific to the context of college enrollment, the cultural capital valued generally is closely pegged to dominant culture norms (Bourdieu, 1977; Lareau & Weininger, 2004; Yosso, 2006). For example a prospective student may be particularly knowledgeable about hip-hop culture. This knowledge, cultural capital, of this genre may be of high value in many venues: *Yahoo!* once hosted a personals ad of a single White male looking for a single White female who, among other qualities, should know the words to at least one rap song. For this young White man, while a non-White was not a suitable mate, a good partner for him had to include knowledge of a rap song in her bundle of cultural capital goods.

In terms of what is valued on a college application, however, knowledge of hip-hop, to be valued, must be imprinted by dominant cultural insignia: an originally produced audio and/or visual media (probably assuming an additional display of competency in classical music); a poem—rap without music; or a proper research paper anchored in fields such as the history, economics, or sociology of hip-hop. While this list is hardly exhaustive, it demonstrates the difficulty that students with interests different from the dominant culture may have in producing an application with the "appropriate" sets of activities and accomplishments to apply to college. In addition to having the "right" set of precollege experiences is the know-how associated with navigating the college process. For first-generation students, regardless of race, this cultural capital by definition is not found in the immediate family and may not be found in the extended family. Therefore, without further social capital, networks that can help improve one's knowledge of a process, a student can be left at sea in spite of his or her abilities.

In considering the racial dimension of a human, social, and cultural capital interlocking framework, Black students tend to overestimate the costs of higher education and underestimate its benefits. The former is largely attributable to the fact that, for many young Blacks, college is a big unknown for the student individually and the family more generally (Freeman, 2005). The "sticker price," tuition and fees, may even exceed family pre-income. Students then experience sticker shock and either pursue cheaper routes or avoid college altogether for fear of incurring insurmountable debt (Heller, 2001). In addition, given low institutional retention and graduation rates, the stories of Blacks who dropped or stopped out of college abound within African American communities. Even with these hurdles aside, students may have a difficult time visualizing themselves attaining money and a certain lifestyle via education. Contemporary tracks such as "School Spirit" found on rapper Kanye West's *The College Dropout* (2004) can contribute to depreciation of the value of college. More broadly, however, the reification of musicians, actors/actresses, and athletes as individuals who have "made it" in the African American community obscures the route college plays in the lives of the not so talented or lucky. Here access to social networks with open dominant cultural capital reserves, ready to be shared, can be helpful in demystifying the process and the payoff.

Young Black Women's Bundles of Human, Social, and Cultural Capital

In this study, the 1988 National Education Longitudinal Study (NELS:88/00) sponsored by the National Center for Education Statistics (NCES) is used to explore the interlocking layers of human, social, and cultural capital of young Black women. The NELS:88/00 contains data from a national sample of 25,000 students in 1,000 schools who were 8th graders in 1988. These students were then followed through four follow-up surveys: 1990, 1992, 1994, and 2000. While dated, NELS:88/00 is the most inclusive NCES dataset spanning student high school careers through college and the workforce (Adelman, 2006). Of the 25,000 students in NELS, 1,475 are African American. Within the African American sample, data on college (any postsecondary) enrollment are available on 1,038 students. Of these students, 582 are female. The college enrollment rate of these women was 62%, compared to a rate for general population of 66.7% and an African American male rate of 53%.

The outcome measure used in this study is college (postsecondary) enrollment: whether a student enrolled in college any time between 1989 and 2000. The binomial logistic regression model included socioeconomic status as a control measure, prior student performance measured by 10th-grade standardized composite math and reading scores, and whether a student was ever held back, in addition to six vectors measuring social and cultural capital at the levels of the family, school, and individual. These vectors are listed in Table 2.2. The family and school social capital proxies used signal conversations, the transmission of knowledge from these entities to the student. Student social capital is the student's report that she has in fact received help

TABLE 2.2
Family, School, and Individual Measures of Social and Cultural Capital

	Social Capital	*Cultural Capital*
Family	• Parent reported discussions regarding school work and college	• Academic artifacts in the home—ownership of dictionaries, books, newspapers, magazines, a designated study area, typewriter, computers, and pocket calculators
School	• School reported student assistance in completing college application and financial aid forms	• School reported percentage of students previously enrolling in college • Teacher reported whether felt made a difference in students' lives
Student	• Student reported receipt of help on college applications, essays, and financial aid forms as indicators • Student perception of peer expectations for his/her continued education after high school • Student reported peers' intentions for postsecondary education	• Units of mathematics • Self-reported SAT or ACT exam taken

with college materials. While peer effects were entered into the model separately, student reports of their peers' collegiate expectations for the student as well as their own expectations are indicators of student peer social networks. Family cultural capital is proxied by family ownership of artifacts students can use in their studies or otherwise to expand their knowledge base. The inclusion of typewriters on this listing implicates the date limitations of NELS:88/00. School cultural capital is measured by the percentage of students in previous years going on to further education in combination with teacher reports of whether they feel they make a difference in the lives of their students. This latter measure was included because, while teachers may value their own education and education for their children personally, they may not be as altruistic in their regard for the children of others (Delpit, 1996). Student cultural capital was measured by units of mathematics, which is the most significant singular predictor of college enrollment, and by the student indication that she took the SAT or ACT. These last two measures are significant as they represent concrete steps toward college enrollment and are distinguishable from college as an abstract aspiration (Freeman, 2005). In consideration of the full human capital model, measures of student prior performance also serve as crude indicators of student human capital, to date.[2]

The models run compared the performance of young Black women to that of young Black men. No statistically significant differences registered between the family and school social and cultural capital given young Blacks. However there were significant differences by gender at the student level.

"Making a Dollar Out of Fifteen Cents"

The distribution of African Americans over socioeconomic quartiles is bottom heavy, with African Americans overly represented among the poor in the United States. Within the NELS dataset, almost twice as many students fall in the first socioeconomic quartile as the second, and almost three times as many as in the highest socioeconomic bracket (see Figure 2.1). Young Black men and women grow up with access to the same school, family, and community amenities to which their socioeconomic statuses make them privy. Yet, young Black women are more adept at minimizing negative influences and are even slightly more likely to make more positive cultural capital investments.

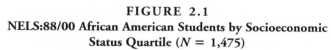

FIGURE 2.1
NELS:88/00 African American Students by Socioeconomic
Status Quartile (*N* = 1,475)

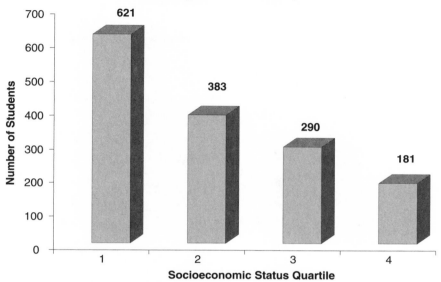

Compared to young Black men, Black women take more units of mathematics and are more likely to take SAT and ACT exams (a 4% difference). This echoes the findings of Gafford Muhammad and Dixson (2007) using a more recent national dataset, the Educational Longitudinal Survey of 2002. Here the statistical depiction of young Black women as engaged and diligent students is more detailed. However, the greatest effects are not in what they do affirmatively, but in that they are less susceptible to negative trappings of the scholastic environment. Socioeconomic status is not a statistically significant predictor of college for young Black women, while of the factors investigated in this model, it is the strongest for Black men (see Table 2.3). For young Blacks, both men and women, peer effects in this model are negative. Yet, peer effects do predict college enrollment or the failure of Black women to enroll. Young Black women are also less likely than Black males to need formal help navigating the college application process (a 24% difference). What seemed to be a positive social cultural factor, reaching out for help, actually is negatively associated with college enrollments. Instead, it acts as a mere indicator of need. Having this need impinges on the college

TABLE 2.3
Predictive Capacity of Social and Cultural Capital on College Enrollment, a Comparison of Young Black Men and Women ($N = 1,038$)

	Men	Women
Socioeconomic Status	+ +	
Prior Achievement		+ +
Held Back	− −	+ +
Family Cultural Capital		
Family Social Capital		
School Cultural Capital		
School Social Capital		
Student Cultural Capital		
Student Social Capital	− −	− −
Peer Effects	+	
Constant		

* Statistically significant at $p < 0.01$.
** Statistically significant at $p < 0.001$.

enrollment probability of young Black women more so than young Black men, but the difference is less than 1%.

The most interesting finding concerns the way in which being held back differentially influences propensity toward college enrollment. Research literature is replete with cautions on the retention of young Black males as it impinges on college enrollment and high school completion (e.g., Ferguson, 2000). Yet, for young Black women, retention seems to be a correcting phase, propelling them forward to further education. This finding is not a mandate to pursue a course of retaining young Black women, however. More needs to be known about differences in the number of times held back, at what grade levels, and for what reasons. It very may well be that grade retention for young Black women in the aggregate is qualitatively different from that of their male counterparts.

Conclusion

Overall, it seems that young Black women are only slightly wiser in how they actively invest, but are significantly less likely to waste the 15 cents they have. They are thereby able to stretch their 15 cents to the value of another's dollar, making college aspirations a reality. Of particular note, the early educational investments of young Black women in their human capital do pay off in additional propensity toward college enrollment. Prior academic performance on examinations, selection of additional units of mathematics, and even corrective performance measures are strong positive predictors of college enrollment for this group. However, measures of social and cultural capital did not register as initially hypothesized. With the exception of student social cultural capital, social and cultural capital investments did not have a statistically significant influence on college enrollment. As for student social cultural capital, the influence is negative, an association that runs contrary to college enrollment. One question this study left unanswered is the degree to which positive and negative social and cultural capital influences cancel each other out in a statistical model. It may be the case that future qualitative research can disentangle the effects of social and cultural capital investments.

Implications for Practice

Students who stand out in classrooms are often the "smartest" or the "baddest." Young Black women tend to be neither. They are, however, among the most diligent. We should not be satisfied by their failure to be attracted to negative trappings. When investments are made in their human capital, the returns are substantial. They not only aspire to go to college, they also enroll, succeed in college, and—with a baccalaureate degree—outpace Black men and White women in earnings. Therefore, in the simplistic terms of human capital investments, it is profitable for teachers, administrators, and counselors to engage this population actively. In particular, these young women should be encouraged to study higher-order mathematics and other academic offerings. Concomitantly, those offerings must be available at the schools they attend. Set those high expectations, and young Black women will pursue them. Historically, they have been the ones to stretch 15 cents to 1 dollar. Let us see what happens when we give them the full attention a dollar can buy.

1. Notes

1. *The Journal of Blacks in Higher Education* reports that the median earnings of Black women in 2004 were 111% of White women's ("Higher Education," 2007,

p. 7). Note that historically, as per education level, African American women are more likely than White women to work outside of the household and to be primary breadwinners in their homes. Black women are less likely to have the luxury of being stay-at-home mothers or part-time workers supplementing their partner's pay (see Giddings, 2006).

2. Human capital and associated theoretical frames tend to be overly simplistic, a factory production model of individuals as they move through systems of education into the labor market. In particular, they fail to account for the interaction of environments on the individual and, more important, the degree to which educational structures reproduce inequality. For the classical critique of human capital theory, see Bowles and Gintis, 1976, 2002.

References

Adelman, C. (2006). *The toolbox revisited: Paths to degree completion from high school through college*. Washington, DC: U.S. Department of Education.

Baron, S., Field, J., & Schuller, T. (2000). *Social capital: Critical perspectives*. Oxford, UK: Oxford University Press.

Becker, G. S. (1993). *Human capital: A theoretical and empirical analysis, with special reference to education*. New York: Columbia University Press.

Bourdieu, P. (1977). *Reproduction in education, society, culture*. Beverly Hills, CA: Sage.

Bowles, S., & Gintis, H. (1976). *Schooling in capitalist America: Educational reform and the contradictions of economic life*. NewYork: Basic Books.

Bowles, S., & Gintis, H. (2002). Schooling in capitalist America revisited. *Sociology of Education, 75*, 1–18.

Coleman, J. S. (1988). Social capital in the creation of human capital. *The American Journal of Sociology, 94*, 95–120.

Delpit, L. (1996). *Other people's children: Cultural conflict in the classroom*. New York: The New Press.

Ferguson, A. A. (2000). *Bad boys: Public schools in the making of Black masculinity*. Ann Arbor, MI: University of Michigan Press.

Freeman, K. (2005). *African-Americans and college choice: The influence of family and school*. Albany, NY: State University of New York Press.

Gafford Muhammad, C., & Dixson, A. (2007). *Benign neglect: An examination of the predictors of college enrollment for African American females*. Paper presented to the American Educational Researchers Association, Chicago, IL.

Giddings, P. (2006). *When and where I enter: The impact of Black women on race and sex in America* (3rd ed.). New York: Amistad.

Heller, D. E. (2001). Trends in the affordability of public colleges and universities: The contradiction of increasing prices and increasing enrollment. In D. E. Heller

(Ed.), *The states and public higher education policy: Affordability, access, and accountability* (pp. 11–38). Baltimore, MD: John Hopkins Press.

Higher education is the major force in closing the Black-White income gap. (2007). *Journal of Blacks in Higher Education, 55*, 6–8.

Lareau, A., & Weininger, E. B. (2004). Cultural capital in educational research: A critical assessment. In D. L. Swartz & V. L. Zolberg (Eds.), *After Bourdieu: Influence, critique, elaboration* (pp. 105–144). Dordrecht, The Netherlands: Kluwer Academic Publishers.

Nulton, L. (1948). Jump rope rhymes as folk literature. *The Journal of American Folklore, 61*, 53–67.

Schuller, T., Baron, S., & Field, J. (2000). Social capital: A review and critique. In S. Baron, J. Field, & T. Schuller (Eds.). *Social capital: Critical perspectives* (pp. 1–38). Oxford University Press.

U.S. Census Bureau (2006). *School enrollment: Social and economic characteristics of students*. Washington, D.C.: Author.

West, K. (2004). School spirit. On *The college drop out* [CD]. Compton, CA: Roc-a-Fella Records.

Yoffie, L. R. C. (1947). Three generations of children's singing games in St. Louis. *The Journal of American Folklore, 60*, 1–51.

Yosso, T. (2006). Whose culture has capital?: A critical race theory discussion of community cultural capital. In A. Dixson & C. K. Rousseau (Eds.), *Critical race theory in education: All God's children got a song* (pp. 167–190). New York: Routledge Press.

PART TWO

THE UNDERGRADUATE EXPERIENCE

3

AN ASSET OR AN OBSTACLE?

The Power of Peers in African American Women's College Transitions

Rachelle Winkle-Wagner

In the interest of better supporting African American students in higher education, scholars have explored topics such as African American student transitions into college, their experiences in college, campus climates related to race or gender, and the influence of peers on academic success. It is no secret that African American students have often reported feelings of isolation on predominantly White postsecondary campuses (Allen, 1992; Feagin, Vera, & Imani, 1998; Winkle-Wagner, in press-a). Yet, many questions remain to be answered about the *reasons* for these feelings of isolation. Some scholars indicate that African American students' feelings of isolation might be related to a hostile racial climate (Hurtado & Carter, 1997) or experiences with discrimination and racism on campus (Feagin et al., 1998). Others have begun exploring the college student transition process, attempting to understand the challenges and issues that students face as they attempt to acclimate to a particular college campus (Goldrick-Rab, Carter, & Winkle-Wagner, 2007). In my own work, I study the tensions African American women face during their time in college, indicating that they often struggle to belong to multiple groups simultaneously, such as their peer groups, families, the larger campus community, and the larger society (Winkle-Wagner, in press-a; in press-b). In this chapter, I consider the connections between students' peers and the campus climate created by students in an attempt to uncover how peer interactions influence the college transition process for African American women.

Review of Literature

There have been numerous attempts to better understand the college student transition process and how this process influences student success. The following is a review of literature related to college student transitions more generally, scholarship regarding the campus climate as it relates to these college transitions, and some of the previous work conducted on peer interactions in college.

College Student Transitions and Campus Climates

In the field of higher education, scholars have asserted recently that the educational system is arranged in a "pipeline" whereby one level of education affects subsequent levels (Pathways to College Network, 2003). The transitions approach, stemming in part from the pipeline idea, explores students' experiences in adjusting to the various levels of education (Goldrick-Rab et al., 2007). This approach generally maintains that a student undergoes a variety of transitions from one stage or time in education to another.

The first year of college is the subject of much attention in the student transitions literature, maintaining the importance of supporting students to help them "integrate" into the campus culture early on in their college careers so that they will continue with their degree programs (Gardner, 2001). In exploring the transition process for students of color, numerous studies focus on the first-year transition and its subsequent impact on student success and chances for persistence (Eimers & Pike, 1997; Hurtado, Carter, & Spuler, 1996). Related to the first-year transition process, family relationships have been identified as an important factor in students' ability to transition into and progress through college (Winkle-Wagner, in press-b; Wintre & Yaffe, 2000). Psychologically based studies that link family relationships to the college transition process often examine students' ability to individuate, or separate themselves from parents (Kalsner & Pistole, 2003; Mattanah, Hancock, & Brand, 2004; Rice, 1992). Yet, strong parental attachment is also associated with successful college adjustment, particularly with academic and emotional adjustment for students of color (Schneider & Ward, 2003; Soucy & Larose, 2000; Strage, 1998).

Another key area in college student transition exploration, for students of color in particular, regards the interactions between the institution and the individual student. In an attempt to understand ways to better serve students from different backgrounds, scholars have begun studying the unique experiences of African American students in higher education (Allen, 1992; Branch, 1998; Feagin et al., 1998; Fries-Britt & Turner, 2002; Harper, Carini, Bridges, & Hayek, 2004; Howard-Hamilton, 2004; Willie, 2003; Winkle-Wagner, in press-a). These scholars have identified factors that influence the college experience for African American students, among them feelings of isolation in predominantly White institutions (PWIs) (Allen, 1992; Feagin et al., 1998) and different types of involvement on campus based on race (Harper et al., 2004). The campus climate literature attempts to uncover the campus environments related to race or gender and the way in which these environments influence students' experiences. Research indicates that many students of color experience racism or a hostile racial climate on campus (Feagin et al., 1998; Hurtado et al., 1996; Hurtado & Carter, 1997; Hurtado, Carter, & Kardia, 1998). Yet, more work is needed. For example, in their work with campus racial climates, Hurtado and Carter (1997) suggest that there is a need for future work that grapples with the subjective reports of students' individual experiences in navigating various campus environments.

The college student experience or campus climate literature is typically only subtly connected to the transitional pipeline. That is, often the transitions literature is relegated to the early or first-year transition process, and the college experience literature is a separate silo related to the subsequent time in college. One needs to bring these lines of work together to examine the larger transition process for students—investigating transitions from the first year through graduation.

By identifying the processes, potential barriers, and supportive elements of this full transition process, one might learn better ways to support students through these transitions, ultimately influencing persistence and students' academic success. Yet, there is relatively little work done specifically on the way that peer interactions influence college transitions, particularly the continued transitions (i.e., not only the first year) of students of color. This chapter begins to fill this gap by examining African American women's reflections on peer interactions and the way that these interactions influence their continued transitions in college.

Peer Influence in College

Peer influences on the college student experience have been studied in multiple ways, although rarely using a transitions framework. Peers are an important part of the college choice-making process. According to the statistical analysis of the NELS dataset, friends' plans are the most important factor in the college-going decisions of minority, low-income, urban youth (Sokatch, 2006). Yet, according to Tierney and Coylar (2005), many other questions remain about the influence of peers on college-going decisions. Once a student is enrolled in college, peer interactions influence many aspects of students' educational experiences, including educational aspirations (Hallinan & Williams, 1990); academic success in college (Harper, 2006); development of identity (Kaufman & Feldman, 2004); and such college student behaviors as involvement in co-curricular organizations (Harper et al., 2004) to name just a few.

Interracial interactions among peers are seen as influential in the academic success of *both* minority and majority group members. For example, in a statistical analysis using the High School and Beyond dataset, Hallinan and Williams (1990) maintain that educational aspirations were influenced positively by interracial peer interactions. According to a multi-institutional, survey-based study of the cognitive outcomes of experiences with diversity in college, informal interactions with diverse peers in college improved educational outcomes (Gurin, Dey, Hurtado, & Gurin, 2002). Yet, there is evidence that while students *experience* diversity, meaning that they have contact with people from different backgrounds from their own (Antonio, 2001), *meaningful* cross-racial interactions rarely occur on most predominantly White campuses (Gurin et al., 2002).

Once students are enrolled in college, peer interaction can be a significant factor in their college success. Through in-depth interviews regarding students' "felt" identities, Kaufman and Feldman (2004) found that students' self-identification with academics or with being smart was heavily affected by their interactions with peers.

While there is a history of work regarding peer influences for African American males in higher education and sociology, very little research addresses African American *women's* peer interactions. For example, anthropologist John Ogbu's work (Fordham & Ogbu, 1986; Ogbu, 1974; Ogbu & Davis, 2003) regarding the "acting White" concept considered the ways that peer groups negatively influenced African American male adolescents' academic success. Yet, more recently, in a multi-institutional study with African American men, Harper (2006) found that peer support actually influenced these men's academic success in positive ways. Prudence Carter (2006) built on and critiqued Ogbu's work in her scholarship about peer group effects on the academic success of African American women. Her findings indicate that, in fact, African American adolescent women do experience different effects of peer relationships from their male counterparts. But, her work focuses primarily on African American female adolescents. A need remains for research highlighting the effects of peer relationships on African American women in college, because peer relationships may affect female students in different ways from how they affect male students. This chapter begins to bridge this gap in the literature, providing insight into the positive and negative effects of peer interactions for African American women in college.

Methodology

The data presented here are part of a larger critical ethnographic study of women's college experiences and identity. The primary research question for this paper was: What affects the early and continued college transitions of first-generation African American women?

Participants

The larger study included 42 women (25 African American, 4 Black-Latina, 2 multiracial, and 11 White), and data were collected for 9 months. For the purposes of this discussion, I focus primarily on the 31 Black[1] women in the study, 25 of whom were first-generation college students, meaning that their parents were not college-educated. Table 3.1 provides a demographic breakdown of these participants.

The majority of these women ($N = 25$) were first-generation students. The 31 participants include women who self-identified "African American" or "Black" as their primary racial classification; those who are multiracial and claim "Black" as one of their racial groups; or women who are Black/Latina and claim "Black" as one of their racial groups. I included the multiracial and Afro-Latina women in this discussion because of their clear self-identification as "Black" and because they typically related to the experiences of the African American women.

The research site was a large, predominantly White, public, Midwestern, Carnegie Research Extensive institution of higher education, called Midwest University (MU).[2] The institution had a relatively low minority population (approximately 9% of the total student population—4% African American, 2% Latino, 3% Asian American).

TABLE 3.1
Demographics of Black Female Participants

	Number of Participants
Race/Ethnicity	
African American	25
Black Latina	4
Multiracial	2
Year in College	
Freshman	6
Sophomore	8
Junior	7
Senior	10
Major by College	
Arts and Sciences	12
Education	4
University Division/Undecided	5
Business and Marketing	6
Health and Recreation	3
Public Policy/Environmental Affairs	1
First-Generation Student	
Students who were first generation	25
Students whose parents had college degrees	6

The study was a qualitative research project, rooted in critical ethno-graphic methods (Carspecken, 1996).[3] Using purposive sampling (Creswell, 1998), I selected African American women (ages 18–22) from three groups on campus for voluntary participation in the study (an early intervention, need-based aid program; a merit-based aid program; and an African American learning community in the residence halls). To recruit the women, I sent e-mails, called, and visited organizational meetings. The participants also began to recruit subsequent participants during the study. I separated the women into 9 focus groups, whose size was determined by the women (e.g., approximately 3–5) and which met biweekly for 9 months.

Focus groups and individual interviews were audiotaped and transcribed verbatim. I coded data from the individual interviews and focus groups to allow themes and subthemes to emerge (Carspecken, 1996). Before the coding process, I used a variety of analysis techniques to delve deeper into the meaning in the women's statements. For example, I used meaning field analysis, developed by Carspecken (1996), to determine the range of possible meanings for each statement. Then, I used a technique called reconstructive horizon analysis (Carspecken, 1996) to elucidate the objective, subjective, normative, and identity claims[4] that were both explicit and implicit within the statements. These techniques deepened the meaning of the codes, and they served as a validation technique to ensure rigor in the analysis process.

I used a variety of validation techniques to ensure that the data analysis was trustworthy such as (Carspecken, 1996): peer debriefing (colleagues reviewed the analysis); member checks (participants reviewed the analyses and the transcripts); and a reflective assessment of my own biases and value orientations.

Findings: The Power of Peers

African American students reported many influences, both positive and negative, on their college transition process. The powerful influence of peers on the college transitions of the African American women involved in this study cannot be underscored enough. Peers can serve as a barrier to doing well in college or as a catalyst and support network. I focus here on peer influences and the way that peers were perceived to be either an asset ("We've Got a Clothesline": Positive Peer Influences) or a barrier (It Can "Ruin Your Entire College Experience": Negative Peer Influences and a Hostile Racial Climate) to African American women's success in college.

"We've Got a Clothesline": Positive Peer Influences

Long-term friendships. Friendships and positive peer relationships were helpful in the women's transition into college. Monica, a sophomore sociology major whose parents were college-educated, remembers, "It wasn't that hard of a transition for me. I don't know if it was because I knew that my family was close by, or I had a lot of friends down here. But, it wasn't that hard for me." Monica came to campus with a couple of longtime childhood friends, and they navigated the campus together. When asked where they felt the safest and most comfortable on campus, the women, both those who were first-generation and those who were not, responded resoundingly like Monica: "Hanging out with friends." Brandi, a close friend of Monica's and a sophomore biochemistry major whose parents held advanced degrees, elaborated on the importance of positive friendships in offering a place where one can be understood on campus: "You can just be yourself I guess. They know you and they know who you are so they don't make assumptions about you, because they know you." Here Brandi underscores the importance of having a place, through her friendship, where she could just be herself and relax. Both Monica and Brandi were involved in a merit-based scholarship program, and they described the importance of their friendship numerous times when discussing their initial and continued transitions through college.

First-generation women also described the importance of positive friendships in helping their transition process and in their persistence decisions. Mercedes and Krystal, who have been part of the same friendship group of six women since middle school, described their friends as a positive influence on both their decision to go to college and their decision to persist. They described numerous times when one of the six women would be ready to leave school, and the others would encourage her to remain or find a way to give her the support she needed, such as encouraging tutoring, studying, and using campus resources. Mercedes, a first-year, first-generation criminal justice major explained, "We got a clothesline, and there's not too many people that's gonna get left behind. Somebody's *fallin'* behind, but they're not gonna get *left* behind." They encouraged each other through college, making intellectuality and learning a positive thing. Mercedes proudly noted, "We are scholars," indicating their self-identification with being smart and placing academics as a priority in their lives. In the peer group of Krystal and Mercedes, being a "scholar" was a positive characteristic, and this encouraged the women to succeed academically. In this case, the peer group to which Mercedes and Krystal belonged provided them a safe place to identify positively as being academically engaged.

Campus involvement and positive peer influences. For African American women, both first-generation and those whose parents were college-educated, involvement in activities on campus facilitated building positive peer relationships. Many of the African American women were involved in organizations that related to their ethnic identity such as the Black Student Union (BSU). These organizations provided a way for Black students to feel the often-lacking sense of belonging on campus. Ryan, a first-generation sopho-more, biochemistry/premedicine major, explained her desire to be involved in the BSU: "I found out that I like being around my own kind." For Ryan, the BSU provided her a space on campus where she did not feel as outnum-bered racially. She continued to explain how involvement in the BSU could help her in the future: "It seems like a pretty good support system. Nice way to network. Good way to say, 'Hey I'm in such and such group,' and then your boss just happens to be in that. Gives you an extra boost." Ryan, like many of the African American women in this study, spoke very positively about the support she received from the BSU. When asked what one of the most important factors was associated with her decision to *stay* in her degree program, she responded simply, "the Black Student Union," indicating that this organization and its positive peer influence were vital components of her transitions throughout college.

Black Greek letter organizations were another source of support and belonging for some of the African American women. For example, Mercedes, who considered leaving school during her first semester, spoke more posi-tively about her campus experience after she joined a Black Greek letter orga-nization. She also stopped talking about leaving school after she became involved in this organization.

While peers, particularly African American peers, were often described as having an important positive influence on success in college, there was a contrary side. Compared to the "clothesline" notion of helping one another through the college transition process, some women said that peer interac-tions could have an equally negative influence on their transition process.

It Can "Ruin Your Entire College Experience": Negative Peer Influences and a Hostile Racial Climate

These positive peer influences garnered from long-term friendships, ethni-cally oriented involvement, and positive relationships built on campus were compared to negative peer influences where peers became a barrier to doing well in college. These negative influences stemmed at times from both the African American peer groups and White peers on campus, inside and out-side of the classroom.

Within-group negative peer influences. Mercedes and Krystal, both having mentioned the vital importance of friendships in their initial and continued college transitions, compared these positive experiences to more negative ones. They lived in the same residence hall, in the African American learning community, on a floor where many of their peers were not doing well in school. Mercedes worried, "It's just like. . . . You can't get nothin' done. I can't even study on that floor." In this case, Mercedes's peers were perceived as a detriment to her academics in college. Sleeping was also an issue on the floor. Mercedes explained how a lack of sleep because of noise on the floor was affecting her:

> Like, I'd try to go to bed like around two o'clock [in the morning], but I wouldn't be asleep, I would just be sitting up there hearing this and hearing that. Looking at the clock—three o'clock, four o'clock, five o'clock, six o'clock. I might fall asleep somewhere during that, but it wasn't for more than an hour. God, it's stressful when you can't sleep.

Krystal, a first-year, first-generation sports management major, maintained that negative peer relationships like the ones that they had on their residence hall floor will "ruin your whole entire college experience." Contrasted with the positive peer group, the peers whom they encountered in their residence hall were detrimental to academic success for both Mercedes and Krystal. Women in other residence halls did not mention the same problems with sleeping and studying in their residence halls. However, three other women involved in the African American living-learning community corroborated the situation Mercedes and Krystal described, indicating that their particular learning community had more of a negative impact on their college success than the positive impact the program intended (Camille, a first-generation junior biology major; Jarena, a first-generation senior apparel merchandising major; and Serena, a first-generation, first-year education major). Both Krystal and Mercedes struggled with these negative influences, ultimately disassociating from their residence hall (i.e., not going to events there, spending less time there, etc.).

Negative interracial interactions. Peers, particularly White peers, could be a barrier, particularly in the classroom. Group class projects emerged as a negative experience time and time again for the African American women, suggesting a hostile racial climate. Often group projects highlighted racism among peers. For example, Claudia, a Black Latina (Puerto Rican, self-identifying Black as one identity), first-generation senior psychology major, said that she felt like she was "untouchable" in the classroom because none of her White peers would sit next to her or be in groups with her. She continued to describe her classroom transition process:

There were moments in my classes where I wanted to kick [the White students] . . . I try to not look at White people and just like hate them for what they are saying. . . . If you were raised in a pattern where you learned to hate minorities, or ignore them, you are gonna grow up with that same feeling.

Claudia has developed a coping mechanism, realizing that some of her peers have negative attitudes toward students of color. This is a sad statement for the general expectations that some African American students may have of White students—that they will often be ignorant and that women of color will simply have to look past that ignorance if they don't want to be angry constantly.

Leila, a sophomore business major whose parents were college-educated, concurred with Claudia's statement, "I hate group projects," describing multiple negative experiences where she felt her peers treating her differently because of her race. One time in particular, Leila was ordered around by a White student. She felt silenced because she had to work with the group, but did not feel as if she could give her opinion: "So, if I say anything, I would be the minority in the group. I'm like, 'okay, well . . .'; they'd be like, 'You can get out of the group.'" These negative experiences with small groups in the classroom were gendered and racialized in ways that made the women feel uncomfortable and that were ultimately detrimental to their experiences in class.

Outside of the classroom, the women also had negative experiences with racial discussions that influenced their continued college transitions. Many racial discussions in mixed racial groups resulted in stereotypes. Tracy, a first-generation sophomore education major, shared, "I hate it when people come up to me and ask, 'So, do Black people do this?' I don't know, I can't speak for every Black person. That's what I tell them now. I'm not the spokesperson for everybody." Tracy's example illustrates how White peers often put African American women in positions of representing their racial group. Leila agreed, continuing, "It irritates me when someone knows about five Black friends and they think they know the whole Black race." Not unlike Tracy's statement, Leila indicated, on campus there are many times when African American women felt like they are the "representatives" of their entire race. In addition, Leila's example implies that these stereotypes and lack of exposure on the part of White students result in undue burdens for

African American students, such as feeling like a representative for an entire group of people.

Camiya, a first-generation sophomore business major, responded to Leila and described her feelings about her White peers: "I think that they really don't know. It's ignorance. 'Cause I've [been] around White people all my life. You know what I'm saying? And they are really curious. Like, they don't know. So, they ask what we think are stupid questions and assume things." Tracy added, "You just gotta keep on goin'." Again, there is an implicit mention of the exhaustion that stems from African American women constantly having to educate their White peers while also trying to learn and navigate the campus experience.

In another example, Michelle, a senior, first-generation, public health major, reflected on her transition process. Michelle's roommates her second year in college were all White. She reflected:

> It was really, really hard. Because they grew up in, like, somewhere weird, like a weird little town off to the side of [the state]. I don't know what it is, but it was one of those little bitty towns somewhere in [the state]. And you know, it was kind of weird like that. And so they had not interacted with Black people at all.

Michelle's experience with her roommates made her feel different and marginalized in what was supposed to be her home, eventually serving as the catalyst for her to move off campus. She felt that her roommates' lack of interaction with people of different racial groups made them less accepting, ultimately making her living experience less comfortable. The discomfort Michelle felt led her to decide to move off campus.

Discussion

Peers can be a barrier or an opportunity, an obstacle or an asset, in the early and continued college transitions of African American women, according to these data. Positive friendships, often long-term relationships that students brought to campus with them, were frequently mentioned as one of *the* primary aids in both the early and continued college transition process for African American women, regardless of their first-generation status. Relationships fostered by student organizations, particularly those that were ethnically or racially related, such as Greek letter organizations or the Black Student Union, were also considered to be a positive factor in the transitions of African American women in this study. Again, this did not differ between those women who were first-generation and those who were not. The data here point to the importance of these organizations in supporting the positive transitions and college success of African American women on predominantly White campuses. More work is needed to identify African American women's reactions to ethnically/racially related involvement on campus and how their previous experiences (e.g., the demographics of their high schools, the demographics of their home communities, etc.) influence their campus involvement or the women's desire to get involved in this way.

On the contrary, negative peer influences adversely affected the African American women's transitions and experiences inside and outside the classroom. At times, these negative peer interactions made learning more difficult, as was the case when women were unable to find groups with which to work in the classroom. Additionally, the women suggested the presence of a hostile racial climate on campus, and this made it more difficult to learn or even to simply feel a part of the campus. Outside the classroom, the African American women often encountered racial ignorance, a lack of racial understanding, or their White peers' lack of exposure to diversity. The women intimated exhaustion with the constant need to deal with these negative experiences, again suggesting a racial campus climate that was neither welcoming nor conducive to the success of African American women and one that made the transition process more burdensome for students of color. Future studies should consider ways to better manage the larger institutional effects of this ignorance or lack of exposure on the part of White students on African American women and White students alike. While these data do consider some of the subjective experiences with a hostile racial climate on campus, more work is needed in this area to understand fully ways to combat this negative campus climate for students of color.

It is noteworthy that, in general, the African American women described *positive* peer influences only with their African American peers. This is not to say that the African American women in this study did not report some negative experiences with their African American peers. But it is remarkable that there were no descriptions of positive peer experiences with White peers. That is, I did not attempt to *highlight* the negative interracial interactions to the exclusion of positive interactions. Rather, the reason there was so much focus on negative interactions is that there was little or no mention of positive interactions with White peers. This is not to say that these positive interactions are not happening. However, this could be a serious indication that positive cross-racial interaction is limited or even nonexistent on this predominantly White campus.

Significant work is needed to uncover ways to encourage positive interracial peer interactions on college campuses. For example, there are attempts on the campus of Midwestern University to create positive discussions on race at the undergraduate level. For example, there is a program, called Discussion on Diversity,[5] that allows multiracial groups to discuss issues of race on and off campus. This program in particular has received national attention and there is evidence that students receive it very positively. However, as the data here suggest, there is a great need for more frequent, intentional, and structured opportunities to discuss race on campus. It should not be the exception so much as the rule that, if students attend a large public university, there are many opportunities for discussions across racial groups.

Conclusion

The powerful influence of peer interactions on the college transition process cannot be underscored enough. Ultimately, students spend more time with peers than they do with any other actors on a college campus. Hence, these peer relationships and interactions could alter a student's college transition process greatly in both the early years and their continued transitions through graduation. For those students who are in racial minority groups on predominantly White campuses, it is vital to address whether these students are experiencing racial misunderstanding or hostility from their peers. If hostility is occurring, it should be one of the primary concerns on a college campus if the successful transition of students of color is at all an institutional goal.

Peer interactions can reflect the interactions happening at other levels on campus such as those between faculty and administrators. That is, administrators and faculty should not neglect to consider how they are modeling behaviors to students. Additionally, some of these important cross-racial conversations can occur deliberately on campus, in and out of the classroom, with the action of faculty, staff, and administrators. If negative peer interactions are commonplace, be they cross-racial or within-racial, students should be included in conversations regarding ways to alter these interactions. According to these data, these interactions may hold the key to successful transitions through college. When it comes to the early and continued transitions of African American women, peer interactions can serve as a "clothesline," pulling women through the transitions process, or as something that will "ruin" their entire college career.

Notes

1. For this paper, African American and Black refer to women who self-identified as African American, Black, Black-Latina, or multiracial, where one of their self-identified racial classifications was Black or African American. The women in the study debated these terms and did not always agree, and I attempt to use both of them to represent this debate.

2. I used pseudonyms for all locations, institutions, and people to protect the confidentiality of participants.

3. Critical methods generally have an advocacy approach that takes into account the history of power and privilege (Carspecken, 1996). Researchers should attempt to understand or learn from participants and should be concerned with oppression and attempting to ameliorate it through the research process itself (Carspecken, 1996). Thus, critical research often has an action component.

4. Objective claims refer to those claims that are generally observable and have multiple access (e.g., third-person claims). Subjective claims refer to the participant's intentions, desires, or feelings. Normative claims refer to value statements or moral/ethical judgments within a statement. Identity claims are a mix of subjective and normative claims to understand what the participant is saying about herself.

5. I have chosen a pseudonym for the program to avoid identifying the research site.

References

Allen, W. R. (1992). The color of success: African-American college student outcomes at predominantly White and historically Black public colleges and universities. *Harvard Educational Review, 62*(1), 26–43.

Antonio, A. L. (2001). Diversity and the influence of friendship groups in college. *The Review of Higher Education, 25*(1), 63–89.

Branch, D. K. (1998). Impressions: African American first-year students' perceptions of a predominantly White university. *The Journal of Negro Education, 67*(4), 416–431.

Carspecken, P. F. 1996. *Critical ethnography in educational research: A theoretical and practical guide.* New York: Routledge.

Carter, P. (2006). Straddling boundaries: Identity, culture, and school. *Sociology of Education, 79:* 304–328.

Creswell, J. W. 1998. *Qualitative inquiry and research design: Choosing among the five traditions.* Thousand Oaks, CA: Sage Publications.

Eimers, M. T., & Pike, G. R. (1997). Minority and nonminority adjustment to college: Differences or similarities? *Research in Higher Education, 38*(1), 77–97.

Feagin, J. R., Vera, H., & Imani, N. (1996). *The agony of education: Black students at White colleges and universities.* New York: Routledge.

Fordham, S., & Ogbu, J. (1986). Black students' school success: Coping with the "burden of 'acting White.'" *The Urban Review, 18*(3), 176–206.

Fries-Britt, S. L., & Turner, B. (2002). Uneven stories: Successful Black collegians at a Black and a White campus. *The Review of Higher Education, 25*(3), 315–330.

Gardner, J. (2001). Focusing on the first-year student. *AGB Priorities, 17,* 1–17.

Goldrick-Rab, S., Carter, D. F., & Winkle-Wagner, R. (2007). What higher education literature has to say about the transition to college. *Teachers College Record, 109*(10), 9–10.

Gurin, P., Dey, E. L., Hurtado, S., & Gurin, G. (2002). Diversity and higher education: Theory and impact of educational outcomes. *Harvard Educational Review, 72*(3), 330–367.

Hallinan, M. T., & Williams, R. A. (1990). Students' characteristics and the peer-influence process. *Sociology of Education, 63*(2), 122–132.

Harper, S. R. (2006). Peer support for African American male college achievement beyond internalized racism and the burden of "acting White." *Journal of Men's Studies, 14*(3), 337–358.

Harper, S. R., Carini, R. M., Bridges, B. K., & Hayek, J. C. (2004). Gender differences in student engagement among African American undergraduates at historically Black colleges and universities. *Journal of College Student Development, 45*(3), 271–284.

Howard-Hamilton, M. F. (Ed.). (2004). Meeting the needs of African American women. *New Directions for Student Services, 104.*

Hurtado, S. & Carter, D. F. (1997). Effects of college transition and perceptions of the campus racial climate on Latino college students' sense of belonging. *Sociology of Education, 70,* 324–345.

Hurtado, S., Carter, D. F., & Kardia, D. (1998). The climate for diversity: Key issues for institutional self-study. *New Directions for Institutional Research, 25*(2), 53–63.

Hurtado, S., Carter, D. F. & Spuler, A. (1996). Latino student transition to college: Assessing difficulties and factors in successful college adjustment. *Research in Higher Education, 37,* 135–157.

Kalsner, L., & Pistole, C. M. (2003). College adjustment in a multiethnic sample: Attachment, separation-individuation, and ethnic identity. *Journal of College Student Development, 44*(1), 92–109.

Kaufman, P., & Feldman, K. A. (2004). Forming identities in college: A sociological approach. *Research in Higher Education, 45*(5), 463–496.

Mattanah, J. F., Hancock, G. R., & Brand, B. L. (2004). Parental attachment, separation-individuation and college student adjustment: A structural equation analysis of mediational effects. *Journal of Counseling Psychology, 51*(2), 213–225.

Ogbu, J. U. (1974). *The next generation: An ethnography of education in an urban neighborhood.* New York: Academic Press.

Ogbu, J. U., & Davis, A. (2003). *Black American students in an affluent suburb: A study of academic disengagement.* Mahwah, NJ: Lawrence Erlbaum.

Pathways to College Network. (2003, August). *A shared agenda: A leadership challenge to improve college access and success.* Washington, DC: Author.

Rice, K. G. (1992). Separation-individuation and adjustment to college: A longitudinal study. *Journal of Counseling Psychology, 39*(2), 203–213.

Schneider, M. E.. & Ward, D. J. (2003). The role of ethnic identification and perceived social support in Latinos' adjustment to college. *Hispanic Journal of Behavioral Sciences, 25*(4), 539–554.

Sokatch, A. (2006). Peer influences on the college-going decisions of low socioeconomic status urban youth. *Education and Urban Society, 39*(1), 128–146.

Soucy, N., & Larose, S. (2000). Attachment and control in family and mentoring contexts as determinants of adolescent adjustment at college. *Journal of Family Psychology, 14*(1), 125–143.

Strage, A. A. (1998). Family context variables and the development of self-regulation in college students. *Adolescence, 33*(129), 17–31.

Tierney, W. G., & Coylar, J. E. (2005). The role of peer groups in college preparation programs. In W. G. Tierney, Z. B. Corwin, & J. E. Coylar (Eds.), *Preparation for college: Nine elements of effective outreach* (pp. 46–48). Albany: State University of New York Press.

Willie, S. S. (2003). *Acting Black: College identity, and the performance of race.* New York: Routledge.

Winkle-Wagner, R. (in press-a). *The unchosen me: The creation of identity, race and gender in college.* Baltimore, MD: The Johns Hopkins University Press.

Winkle-Wagner, R. (in press-b). The perpetual homelessness of college experiences: The tensions between home and campus for African American women. *The Review of Higher Education.*

Wintre, M. G., & Yaffe, M. (2000). First-year students' adjustment to university life as a function of relationships with parents. *Journal of Adolescent Research, 15*(1), 9–37.

4

AFRICAN AMERICAN FEMALE STUDENTS AT HISTORICALLY BLACK COLLEGES

Historical and Contemporary Considerations

Marybeth Gasman

Issues of racial equality have long received special attention at historically Black colleges and universities (HBCUs). One consequence of this focus, however, is that gender equality issues are sometimes swept under the rug—rarely discussed, except among a small group of feminists (Cole & Guy-Sheftall, 2003). In the words of Black feminist scholar Patricia Hill Collins (Hill Collins, 1999), many Black college women have found themselves in the position of "outsider-within"—meaning that their gender puts them in a disadvantaged position within the racialized Black college community.

This chapter examines the historical and contemporary experiences of Black female students at HBCUs using a gender lens (Hess, Lorber, & Ferree, 1998). Beginning with the pejorative treatment of Black female college students by White missionaries in the 19th century, moving to the often invisible role of Black female students in the 1960s campus and civil rights protests (invisible due to the male domination of most civil rights activities), and concluding with an exploration of the lives and aspirations of Black female students in the current day, I illuminate Black female student experiences through historical inquiry.

The Beginnings of Black Colleges

Most Black colleges were founded in the aftermath of the Civil War, with the exception of three in the North: Lincoln and Cheney universities in Pennsylvania and Wilberforce in Ohio (Anderson, 1988). With the end of the Civil War, the daunting task of providing education to more than 4 million formerly enslaved Blacks was shouldered by both the federal government, through the Freedman's Bureau, and many northern church missionaries (Anderson, 1988). As early as 1865, the Freedmen's Bureau began establishing Black colleges, resulting in staff and teachers with primarily military backgrounds. During this period, most Black colleges were colleges in name only; like many White colleges in their infancy, these institutions generally provided primary and secondary education. From their beginnings, most Black colleges, unlike their historically White counterparts, provided co-educational training. White missionaries and Whites in general saw Black women, like Black men, as potential workers in need of training (Cross Brazzell, 1992; Watson & Gregory, 2005).

The benevolence of the White missionaries was tinged with self-interest and, sometimes, racism (Anderson, 1988; Cross Brazzell, 1992). The missionaries' goal in establishing these colleges was to Christianize the freedmen (i.e., convert formerly enslaved people to *their* brand of Christianity). And while some scholars see the missionaries' actions as largely well meaning (Jencks & Riesman, 1968), many others do not (Anderson & Moss, 1999; Watkins, 2001). According to a more radical group of scholars, the idea of a Black menace was foremost in the minds of these missionaries, who believed that education would curb the "savage" tendencies of the former slaves but should not lead to full-blown social equality (Anderson, 1988; Watkins, 2001). The education provided to Black college students was a mixture of liberal arts and industrial training: classical texts were taught side by side with manual labor skills for men and household duties for women, both for their own homes as well as for those White homes in which they might work. Unlike many White women, Black women did not have the option of not working outside the home. Many Black colleges also provided teacher training for both men and women (Anderson, 1988).

With the passage of the second Morrill Act in 1890, the federal government again took an interest in Black education, establishing public land-grant Black colleges and universities. This act stipulated that those states practicing segregation in their public colleges and universities would forfeit federal funding unless they established agricultural and mechanical institutions for the Black population. Despite the wording of the Morrill Act, which called for the equitable division of federal funds, these newly founded institutions received less money than did their White counterparts and thus had inferior facilities (Gasman, 2007). Just as before the Act, women who attended these schools learned household duties, such as how to cook, clean, make brooms, and sew. On the other hand, men were trained in brick making and laying, farming, blacksmithing, and other forms of manual labor (Spivey, 2006). These kinds of industrial curricula were the norm for women and men at many private Black colleges as well, causing Black intellectuals, such as W. E. B. Du Bois and Mary Church Terrell, to call for more classically focused curricula at these institutions. Black feminists today argue that an industrial curriculum for women, including classes in millinery, sewing, cooking, and household management, was central to White control of Black women. This curriculum, according to some Black scholars, perpetuated the Black mammy image that Whites found comforting. The Black woman (the Black college student) was, in the eyes of many Whites, "a harmless, ignorant woman whose main pleasure was to take care of them" (Collins, 2001, p. 33).

However, it was not until the turn of the 20th century that most Black colleges seriously began to provide a college-level, liberal arts education (Anderson, 1988). Institutions such as Fisk in Tennessee, Dillard in Louisiana, and Howard in Washington, D.C., exemplified this approach, schooling their male and female students in the classics. For the most part, these colleges prepared women for teaching positions in schools and colleges and for public service. However, it is important to note that, much like their White counterparts, these women were expected to enroll in home economics courses to complement their academic skills.

During the early years of Black colleges, female students were sheltered by the mostly White female administration; their lives were shaped by institutional policies designed to control their behavior (Perkins, 1996; Watson & Gregory, 2005). In the eyes of the White missionaries, Black women had been stripped of their feminine virtue by the experiences of slavery and as such had to be purified before they could assume the responsibilities of the home (Cross Brazzell, 1992; Gray White, 1999). Typically, during the late 1880s, female Black college students were not allowed to leave the campus without a member of the administration escorting them. By contrast, men were free to come and go as they pleased. At most institutions, the dean of women lived on campus to watch over the fragile and impressionable young college girls (Bell Scott, 1997; Perkins, 1996). The dean of men, on the other hand, lived off campus, as did the other upper-level administrators (Bell Scott, 1997; Perkins, 1996). During the mid-1920s, many female students at Black colleges and universities urged campus administrators to grant them greater autonomy, noting that it would help them learn self-reliance—a skill they saw as essential to assuming leadership roles (Perkins, 1996). These same women fought vehemently against the repressive religious customs used to rear their race and gender (Watson & Gregory, 2005). White and Black male administrators, many of whom were also ordained Baptist ministers, generally imposed these practices. In particular, the administrators often used the philosophies of St. Paul, an apostle of Jesus, as an excuse to relegate women to second-class status. Women were told that, according to the Bible, patient waiting was to be held above the development of one's talents (Watson & Gregory, 2005). For example, at Howard University, during the 1920s and 1930s, President Mordecai Johnson fought vehemently with Lucy Diggs Slowe, the dean of women, over women's equality. Slowe demanded that the female students at Howard have living conditions equal to those of the men, but to no avail with Johnson. It is interesting to note that Johnson was an ordained Baptist minister. Moreover, in one instance, Slowe represented several female students who had been sexually harassed by a Black male professor. As a result, she received a letter attacking her credibility and that of the students. During Johnson's presidency, despite his amazing skill at institution building, this type of interaction was a common occurrence (Bell Scott, 1997; Eisenmann, 2001; Gasman, 2006; Nidiffer, 1999).

In spite of the heavy hand of religion and the resulting sexism, Black colleges during the late 1800s and early 1900s offered a surprising number of opportunities for Black female students to participate in traditionally male activities. For example, at Talladega College, women were able to join the rifle club (Anderson, 1988; Thelin, 2004). On the other hand, women participated in social service sororities such as Alpha Kappa Alpha and Delta Sigma Theta (Giddings, 1988; Parker, 1978). While sometimes focused on the superficial aspects of appearance and socialization, these organizations were also active in suffrage and civil rights activities as well as other national causes (Gasman, 2005, 2006).

During the 1950s and early 1960s, Black women on Black college and university campuses were instrumental in the Civil Rights Movement. Women at both Bennett and Spelman colleges participated in sit-ins and lunch counter demonstrations (Brown, 1998; Lefever, 2005). The administrators of these women's colleges, now Black rather than White, were, by and large, supportive of the students' actions. However, this was not the case at all Black colleges and universities. At some public Black institutions, which were under the close supervision of state government authorities, administrators declined to help both male and female student protesters who landed in jail (Williamson, 2004).

Many of these young HBCU women were fearless, working diligently to make change within their communities and in the country as a whole (Cole & Guy-Sheftall, 2003). For example, Barbara Harris and Diane Nash, both Fisk University students, were jailed, along with 63 other male and female students who protested Nashville's segregated lunch counters. Although they were offered an opportunity to make bond (at $100 each), they chose to go to jail because, in their minds, paying the bond would be a capitulation to the South's Jim Crow government (Ashley & Williams, 2004; Cole & Guy-Sheftall, 2003; Gasman, 2007). Ironically, as these female students were fighting on behalf of civil rights, their college administrations were still treating them as fragile accessories to men. For example, at the same time that Bennett College students were marching in the streets and attempting to desegregate lunch counters, they were required to take a course, called the "The Art of Living," that focused on becoming a successful homemaker (Bell Scott, 1979, 1997).

In the early 1970s, Gurin and Epps (1975) completed a research study that sought to understand the advantages and disadvantages gained by Black male and female students at HBCUs. Surveying 5,000 African American students, this study was comprehensive and its results compelling. The researchers found that undergraduate women at HBCUs were considerably disadvantaged. In particular, the educational and career goals of female students were significantly lower than those of their male peers. Not only were these Black women less likely to aspire to the Ph.D., but they also were more likely to opt for low-prestige careers in the female sector of the nation's job market (e.g., teaching and the health professions). This seminal research also showed that the patriarchal environments at many HBCUs compounded the problem (Gurin & Epps, 1975; Harper, Carini, Bridges, & Hayek, 2004).

Other researchers have found that social passivity and disengagement on the part of Black women, most likely caused by institutional environments, helped explain why they did not have higher career aspirations (Bell Scott, 1979; Hine, 1999; Hine & Thompson, 1999; Thompson, 1973; Washington & Newman, 1991).

Scholars in the mid-1980s found that, although women were actively engaged in the classroom and in extracurricular activities, they spent less time interacting with individual faculty members (Bonner, 2001). This practice could result in fewer discussions about graduate school and less support for non-female career fields. Moreover, Fleming (1984) found that men at Black colleges were dominant in both the classroom and social settings, and that women were less competitive. In Fleming's own works, "the big issue for women on black campuses is their fear of using assertive skills" (p. 145). More recently, researchers have shown more equal gains for men and women from the HBCU experience (Bonner, 2001; Harper et al., 2004). It appears that women have become less passive and have overcome some of the barriers placed before them. However, an atmosphere persists at many campuses that encourages women to cede to their male counterparts in class discussions and student leadership positions (Bonner, 2001; Guy-Sheftall, 1982; Harper et al., 2004).

Studies also have shown that African American female students at HBCUs feel a higher level of anxiety about their academic performance than do their male counterparts (Bonner, 2001; Fleming, 1984). In addition, when surveyed, they expressed feeling less competent than males. Other studies have revealed that female students were more willing to take on positions and roles that made them seem less competent to avoid threatening their male peers (Washington & Newman, 1991). According to Fleming (1984), at Black colleges,

> Women who become a little more assertive in college, but not as much as men, suffer from feelings of unhappiness . . . [and] women who give little thought to suppressing assertiveness find that they are less popular by the senior year. It looks, then, as if women invest in not asserting themselves so that they can maintain the approval of men. Perhaps this is our root of female competence anxiety. (p. 145)

Despite these feelings of insecurity, women's academic performance at HBCUs outpaces that of Black males. A recent study showed that at most

HBCUs, the percentage of Black women on the honor roll was larger than the percentage of women enrolled at the institutions. For example, at Clark Atlanta University in 2005, women accounted for 69% of the student body but made up 84% of the dean's list. Likewise, at Howard University, women made up 60% of the student body but accounted for 70% of the honor roll. On average, the proportion of women on dean's lists at HBCUs exceeded their enrollment by 10% ("Women Dominate," 1995).

Currently, the nation's HBCUs enroll approximately 250,000 African American students, with a large proportion attending private, four-year institutions. Black women make up the majority of the student population at most Black colleges. For example, at Dillard University, women account for almost three-quarters of the student body. Moreover, at Fisk and Hampton universities, women make up 70% of all students enrolled. According to a *Journal of Blacks in Higher Education* article ("Women Dominate," 1995), even at Tuskegee University, "which is known for its strong programs in the agricultural sciences (a discipline not considered to be a favorite course of study among women), women are now a majority of the student body" (p. 46). When looked at as a whole, HBCUs grant roughly 28% of bachelor's degrees, 15% of master's degrees, 9% of doctoral degrees, and 15% of professional degrees awarded to African Americans (U.S. Department of Education, National Center for Education Statistics [NCES], 2003). Black women outpace Black men at all educational levels. Despite generally favorable statistics for degree attainment for women, the majority of these degrees are in traditionally female-dominated programs. Over 70% of Black women's degrees earned at HBCUs are in the health professions or education (Hayes & Boone, 2001). Black women, like White women, hold positions in service areas and are less likely to work in the sciences. Here certain Black colleges are trying to make gains. For example, of the Black women who enter graduate programs in the sciences, 50% are from Spelman and Bennett colleges—schools that have special programs preparing their students for scientific fields (United Negro College Fund [UNCF], n.d.). Moreover, HBCUs represent the top 20 institutions overall in the placement of Black women in graduate programs in the sciences at all U.S. institutions of higher education (*Diverse Issues in Higher Education*, from www.diverseeducation.com, March 15, 2007). Xavier University in New Orleans, in particular, sends more Black women into U.S. medical schools than does any other institution in the country (UNCF, n.d.).

Some recent research has shown that Black college and university women are now selecting majors that were once exclusively male—including science, technology, engineering, and math (STEM). And Black colleges are having tremendous success in their efforts to graduate Black women. For example, according to 2003 data from the Department of Education Integrated Postsecondary Education Data System (IPEDS) survey, of all African American female bachelors degrees conferred, Black colleges produce 38% in the biological sciences, 41% in chemistry, 40% in computer science, 40% in math, and 40% in physics (Gasman et al., 2007). Given their lack of financial resources, it is downright astonishing that Black colleges have such great success in educating African American women (Kim & Conrad, 2006). There is little empirical research, however, that captures the success rates of Black colleges in STEM or other disciplines.

In moving forward with research on African American women enrolled at Black colleges, we need to ask more theoretical questions. What existing gender theories can be applied to the lives of women at Black colleges? Why were certain kinds of education and particular roles deemed appropriate for Black college women? How does the treatment of Black women at Black colleges reflect a difference in how Black and White women were (and are) seen in society? How have gender disparities played out at Black colleges? A number of talented female scholars have explored issues pertaining to African American women in higher education. To respect and appreciate the role Black female students have played at Black colleges, it is imperative that we have richer research in this area—research that contextualizes these women within the larger Black college context, and smaller, individual investigations that delve deeply into these women's actions.

References

Anderson, E., & Moss, A. (1999). *Dangerous donations. Northern philanthropy and Black education, 1902–1930.* Columbia, MO: University of Missouri Press.

Anderson, J. (1988). *The education of Blacks in the south, 1860–1935.* Chapel Hill, NC: University of North Carolina Press.

Ashley, D., & Williams, J. (2004). *I'll find a way or make one. A tribute to historically Black colleges and universities.* New York: Amistad Publishing.

Bell Scott, P. (1979). "Schoolin' respectable" ladies of color: Issues in the history of Black women's higher education. *Journal of National Association of Women's Deans and Advisors of Colored Schools,* 22–28.

Bell Scott, P. (1997), To keep my self-respect: Dean Lucy Diggs Slowe's 1927 memo-randum on sexual harassment of Black women. *National Women's Studies Association Journal, 9.*

Bonner, F. (2001). Addressing gender issues in the historically Black college and university community: A challenge and call to action. *The Journal of Negro Education, 70*(3), 176–191.

Brown, L. B. (1998). *The long walk: The story of the presidency of Willa B. Player at Bennett College.* Danville, VA: Bennett College Women's Leadership Institute.

Cole, J. B., & Guy-Sheftall, B. (2003). *Gender talk: The struggle for women's equality in African American communities.* New York: Random House.

Collins, A. C. (2001). Black women in the academy: An historical overview. In R. O. Mabokela & A. L. Green (Eds.), *Sisters of the academy. Emergent Black women scholars in higher education* (pp. 29–42). Sterling, VA: Stylus.

Cross Brazzell, J. (1992). Bricks without straw: Missionary-sponsored Black higher education in the post-emancipation era. *Journal of Higher Education, 63*(1), 26–49.

Eisenmann, L. (2001). Creating a framework for interpreting U.S. women's educational history: Lessons from historical lexicography. *History of Education, 30*(5), 453–470.

Fleming, J. (1984). *Blacks in college.* San Francisco, CA: Jossey-Bass.

Gasman, M. (2005). Sisters in service: African American sororities and the philanthropic support of education. In A. Walton (Ed.), *Women, philanthropy, and education* (pp. 194–214). Bloomington, IN: Indiana University Press.

Gasman, M. (2006). *Swept under the rug: An examination of research on gender and the history of Black colleges.* Paper presented at the annual meeting of the History of Education Society.

Gasman, M. (2007). *Envisioning Black colleges: A history of the United Negro College Fund.* Baltimore, MD: Johns Hopkins University Press.

Gasman, M. (forthcoming). Eyes firmly fixed on the prize: African American fraternities and sororities and their role in the Civil Rights Movement. In M. W. Hughley & G. S. Parks (Eds.), *Empirical studies of Black Greek letter organizations.* Louisville, KY: University of Kentucky.

Gasman, M., Perna, L. W., Yoon, S., Drezner, N., Lundy-Wagner, V., & Gary, S. (2007, March). *Black women in STEM at historically Black colleges and universities.* Paper presented at the annual meeting of the American Educational Research Association, Chicago, IL.

Giddings, P. (1988). *In search of sisterhood: Delta Sigma Theta and the challenge of the Black sorority movement.* New York: William Morrow, 1988.

Gray White, D. (1999). *Too heavy a load: Black women in defense of themselves, 1894–1994.* New York: W.W. Norton.

Gurin, P., & Epps, E. (1975). *Black consciousness: Identity and achievement*. New York: John Wiley & Sons.

Guy-Sheftall, B. (1982). Black women and higher education: Spelman and Bennett colleges revisited. *The Journal of Negro Education, 51*(3), 278–287.

Harper, S., Carini, R., Bridges, B., & Hayek, J. (2004). Gender differences in student engagement among African American undergraduates at historically Black colleges and universities. *Journal of College Student Development, 45*(3), 271–284.

Hayes, B., & Boone, L. R. (2001). Women's health research at historically Black colleges and universities. *American Journal of Health Studies, 17*(2), 59–65.

Hess, B., Lorber, J., & Ferree, M. (Eds). (1998). *The gender lens: Re-visioning gender*. Lanham, MD: AltaMira Press.

Hill Collins, P. (1999). *Black feminist thought: Knowledge, consciousness, and the politics of empowerment*. New York: Taylor & Francis.

Hine, D. (1999). *Black women in America*. New York: Oxford University Press.

Hine, D., & Thompson, K. (1999). *A shining thread of hope. A history of Black women in America*. New York: Broadway Books.

Jencks, C., & Riesman, D. (1968). *The academic revolution*. New York: Doubleday Books.

Kim, M., & Conrad, C. F. (2006). The impact of historically Black colleges and universities on the academic success of African American students. *Research in Higher Education, 47*, 399–427.

Lefever, H. G. (2005). *Undaunted by the fight: Spelman College and the Civil Rights Movement*. Macon, GA: Mercer University Press.

Nidiffer, J. (1999). *Pioneering deans: More than wise and pious matrons*. New York: Teachers College Press.

Parker, M. (1978). Alpha Kappa Alpha: In the eye of the beholder. Washington, DC: Alpha Kappa Alpha Sorority.

Perkins, L. (1996). Lucy Diggs Slowe: Champion of the self-determination of African American women in higher education. *The Journal of Negro History, 81*(1/4), 89–104.

Spivey, D. (2006). *Schooling for the new slavery: Black industrial education, 1868–1915*. New York: New World Press.

Thelin, J. (2004). *A history of American higher education*. Baltimore, MD: Johns Hopkins University Press.

Thompson, D. (1973). *Private Black colleges at the crossroads*. Westport, CT: Greenwood Press.

United Negro College Fund (UNCF) Web site. (n.d.). Retrieved June 28, 2007, from http://www.uncf.org

U.S. Department of Education, National Center for Education Statistics (NCES). (2003). *Digest of education statistics*. Retrieved June 29, 2007, from http://nces.ed.gov/

Washington, V., & Newman, J. (1991). Setting our own agenda: Exploring the meaning of gender disparities among Blacks in higher education. *The Journal of Negro Education, 60*(1), 19–35.

Watkins, W. (2001). *The White architects of Black education: Ideology and power in America, 1865–1954.* New York: Teachers College Press.

Watson, Y., & Gregory, S. T. (2005). *Daring to educate: The legacy of early Spelman college presidents.* Sterling, VA: Stylus.

Williamson, J. (2004). "This has been quite a year for heads a falling": Institutional autonomy in the civil rights era. *History of Education Quarterly, 44*(4), 489–511.

"Women dominate the honor rolls at Black colleges." (1995). *Journal of Blacks in Higher Education, 6,* 46–47.

5

AFRICAN AMERICAN WOMEN AT HIGHLY SELECTIVE COLLEGES

How African American Campus Communities Shape Experiences

MaryBeth Walpole

A lthough discrimination was outlawed in higher education in 1950 (*McLaurin v. Oklahoma State Regents*, 339 U.S. 637, 1950; *Sweatt v. Painter*, 339 U.S. 629, 1950), and despite the substantial progress that began following those cases and the epic 1954 Supreme Court ruling in *Brown v. Board of Education*, African Americans remain decidedly underrepresented on the nation's campuses and continue to lag behind Whites and Asian Americans in college enrollment, academic achievement, and degree attainment (Carter & Wilson, 1996; Freeman, 1997, 1999; U.S. Department of Education, National Center for Education Statistics [NCES], 2005; Nettles, 1991; Wilson, 1998). African American women attend college and graduate at rates higher than those of their male peers (U.S. Department of Education, NCES, 2005), but insufficient research has focused on African American women's experiences (Haniff, 1991; Matthews & Jackson, 1991). Overall, research on African American college students has indicated that, although the majority of these students attend predominantly White institutions (PWIs), they are less satisfied, experience significant social isolation,

The author would like to acknowledge Educational Testing Service for its funding and support of this study.

and are less likely to finish than either White students or African American students who attend historically Black colleges and universities (HBCUs) (Allen, 1988, 1991; Astin 1993; Fleming, 1984; Pascarella & Terenzini, 2005; Thompson & Fretz, 1991; White, 1998).

African Americans attending highly selective institutions persist in higher percentages than do African Americans attending less-selective institutions, and most of those highly selective colleges and universities are residential with a liberal arts focus in the undergraduate curriculum. Elite liberal arts colleges and universities have consistently produced more positive educational, affective, and earnings outcomes (Astin, 1999) than have less selective institutions. However, African Americans often experience isolation and racism in these types of elite education settings (Alexander-Snow, 1999; Bowen & Bok, 1998; Cary, 1991; Graham, 1995). In an effort to examine more closely the impact of predominately White, highly selective institutions on African American women, this study qualitatively investigated the experiences of 19 female African American college students at 2 highly selective, predominately White institutions.

Literature Review

African Americans are less likely to enroll in or graduate from college than are their White peers, although African American women enroll and graduate in higher numbers than do African American men (U.S. Department of Education, NCES, 2005). Furthermore, even though the benefits of HBCUs are well documented, the majority of African Americans attend PWIs (Allen, 1988, 1991; Astin 1993; Fleming, 1984; Pascarella & Terenzini, 2005; Thompson & Fretz, 1991; White, 1998). As stated earlier, however, African American students at PWIs are less satisfied, more socially isolated, and less likely to persist than are those at HBCUs (Allen, 1988, 1991; Astin 1993; Cabrera, Nora, & Terenzini, 1999; D'Augelli & Hershberger, 1993; Davis et al., 2004; Fleming, 1984; Pascarella & Terenzini, 2005; Thompson & Fretz, 1991; White, 1998). The social isolation resulting from being a minority student on a campus may be compounded by low levels of involvement in student activities, in part because the activities offered are less appealing to African Americans (Davis, 1991; Taylor & Olswang, 1997). There is evidence, however, that involvement in campus activities and contact with faculty may be fostered by particular campuses and may be facilitated by prior experience in White majority settings (MacKay & Kuh, 1994; Thompson & Fretz, 1991).

Moreover, some research has found positive benefits for African American students attending PWIs. Several researchers believe that African Americans who attend PWIs have high career and educational aspirations (Allen & Haniff, 1991; Jackson & Swan, 1991). Furthermore, those African American students who do persist and graduate from PWIs have high incomes and access to valuable networks (Bowen & Bok, 1998; Braddock & McPartland, 1988).

In part to combat the isolation and racism present on many predominantly White campuses, African American students often socialize with other African American students and participate in student clubs and groups that focus on African American culture (Allen, 1992; Bennett, 1998). These socialization patterns provide fictive kinship (Bennett, 1998), which assists students in feeling comfortable and integrated on campus, and such integration may be crucial for persistence (Tinto, 1987). However, these patterns also may provide students with further struggle and complexity in negotiating membership within the African American community (White, 1998).

African Americans attending elite preparatory high schools or universities have experienced significant difficulties and isolation (Alexander-Snow, 1999; Cary, 1991; Graham, 1995; Horvat & Antonio, 1999). However, one study indicates that African American students who attend highly selective colleges and universities are more likely to persist than students who attend less selective institutions and have very successful outcomes (Bowen & Bok, 1998). This may be, in part, because highly selective colleges and universities facilitate working in highly paid positions or entering prestigious graduate schools for all students (Domhoff, 1983; Hoffnung & Sack, 1981; Kingston & Lewis, 1990; Kingston & Smart, 1990; Solmon, 1975; Useem & Karabel, 1986). These institutions also reinforce upper-class values and social ties and may inculcate certain cultural attributes and values in students who attend them (Domhoff, 1983; Katchadourian & Boli, 1994; Kingston & Lewis, 1990; Useem & Karabel, 1986; Zweigenhaft, 1993). These cultural attributes, values, and ties constitute cultural and social capital specific to the White middle to upper-middle classes, however, and this dominance of White upper-class values often contributes to African American students' isolation (Cary, 1991; Graham, 1995).

Scholarship focused specifically on African American women is limited, and scholars have called for more research on African American women (Haniff, 1991; Matthews & Jackson, 1991). However, several important points from the existing literature on African American women have emerged to inform this study. Although African American women at PWIs were socially isolated, Fleming (1984) found that these women more fully developed their intellectual skills than did women at HBCUs. She attributed this to their ability to develop what she termed "assertiveness" because there were fewer dominant African American men on PWI campuses. However, Jackson (1998) found that African American women at co-educational PWIs focused on their racial identities and did not develop their gender identities as fully as women at HBCUs. She attributed this finding to the fact that the co-educational PWIs focused support on African American students and on women students, but did not address the unique needs of students who were both. Moreover, research on African American college women's motivations found that these women focused on the economic benefits of their education, for themselves and their families, and focused on their education as a means of providing services to their communities (Hamilton, 1996).

Also informing this study is the growing debate regarding the importance of class within the African American community (Conley, 1999; Graham, 1999; Pattillo-McCoy, 1999; West, 1994; Wilson, 1980). The African American middle class is growing rapidly, and recent work describes and examines this growing sector of society (Conley, 1999; Graham, 1999; Pattillo-McCoy, 1999). These authors have found that maintaining loyalty and ties, as well as "giving back," to the African American community are extremely important to this sector (Graham, 1999; Pattillo-McCoy, 1999). According to Graham and Pattillo-McCoy, maintaining loyalty to the African American community included discouraging interracial marriage. Religious and civic connections provided forums for both giving back and maintaining ties to the community. Research also uncovered the importance of extended family networks in maintaining middle-class status for African Americans (Conley, 1999; Pattillo-McCoy, 1999).

College attendance and degree completion has long been viewed as critical for social mobility (DiMaggio & Mohr, 1985; Karabel, 1972; Karabel & Astin, 1975; Pascarella & Terenzini, 2005) and has been important in the growth of the African American middle class (Conley, 1999; Pattillo-McCoy, 1999). As has been found in research on White students and White middle-to upper-class cultural capital, perhaps these highly selective institutions can inculcate and reinforce cultural attributes and values specific to the African American middle and upper-middle classes. Recent work documenting the culture and values of the African American middle and upper-middle classes emphasizes loyalty, kinship, and contributing to the community, commonly known as "giving back" (Conley, 1999; Graham, 1999; Pattillo-McCoy, 1999). Transmission of these values may occur through socializing and participating in culturally specific groups and clubs, which researchers have documented among African American students (Allen, 1992; Bennett, 1998). These socialization patterns also may provide access to social capital for students who participate in them. In this way, these socialization patterns may serve a function beyond providing comfort and integration in isolating, and often racist, environments. More research is needed, then, on the highly successful African American women on these elite campuses, how they cope with the isolation, and how their interactions within the college environment may inculcate middle- and upper-class values and how students' values shape their decisions.

Conceptual Framework

Bourdieu (1977, 1990, 1994) uses the concepts of cultural capital and habitus within a particular field, or context, to explain the ways in which societal structures and opportunities combine with individual aspirations to reproduce the existing social structure. In addition to economic capital, each social class possesses social and cultural capital, which parents pass on to their children as attitudes, preferences, and behaviors that are invested for social profits (LaMont & Lareau, 1988). People from the same social class also have common perceptions of strategies for attaining the social profits they desire, identified as a person's habitus (Bourdieu, 1977). Habitus acts as a web of perceptions regarding the possible and appropriate action to take in a particular setting and to achieve a particular goal. These perceptions are shaped by a person's cultural background and values, which are part of social class.

Education in this framework is most useful for its conversion potential. Scholars have shown that one makes educational decisions and choices within the context of one's habitus in an attempt to accumulate capital that may be converted at a future date in pursuit of educational and occupational gains (Lareau, 1993; MacLeod, 1987; McDonough, 1997). An education from a highly selective college or university is an investment that is uniquely capable of converting to higher educational and occupational gains because the retention and graduation rates at such institutions are extremely high (Astin, 1999; Bowen & Bok, 1998), as are the rates of admission to prestigious graduate programs and well-paid occupations (Domhoff, 1983; Hoffnung & Sack, 1981; Kingston & Lewis, 1990; Kingston & Smart, 1990; Solmon, 1975; Useem & Karabel, 1986; Zweigenhaft, 1993).

In translating Bourdieu's concepts into the U.S. context, scholars have worked to incorporate the duality of race and class into their understandings of social status and social class (Davis, 1998, Horvat, 2000; Horvat & Antonio, 1999; MacLeod, 1987; McDonough, Antonio, & Trent, 1997). Researchers examining race and class in educational decisions have found that African Americans' unique cultural capital and habitus have affected students' high school and college experiences (Horvat, 2000; Horvat & Antonio, 1999), and students' decisions about high school curricular offerings and college choice (MacLeod, 1987; McDonough et al., 1997; Walpole et al., 2005). Furthermore, Davis (1998) posited that HBCUs transmit specific types of cultural and social capital to the students who attend.

While attempting to incorporate the duality of race and class, researchers have failed to consider sufficiently the effects of gender. In the context of the U.S. social structure, gender contributes additional complexity to status considerations. Gender within these highly selective colleges may be of particular importance because many highly selective colleges and universities were men's colleges until relatively recently. Gender also plays a role in the conversion of such an investment because there are still occupational fields and positions to which few women gain access and which may be difficult for women to penetrate, particularly African American women (Jackson, 1998). Furthermore, gender and educational outcomes are powerfully linked within the African American community, with African American women being more likely to enroll in college and to receive a degree than are African American men (Fleming, 1984; Jackson, 1998; U.S. Department of Education, NCES, 2005).

Methodology

Qualitative methodology and grounded theory are particularly suited for exploratory studies and can provide significant insight into and understanding of how individuals derive meaning from experiences such as college, particularly within a specific context such as a highly selective PWI (Bogdan & Biklen, 2003). Data for this study came from a larger project of African American and White women on four college campuses. The current study used interview data to focus on African American female students' social experiences on two highly selective college campuses. The study specifically investigated how the students' cultural capital and habitus shaped their social experiences and the role of the African American campus communities in those experiences.

Data come from in-depth interviews with 19 African American females on 2 highly selective campuses. The two campuses were similar in that they were two of the most selective institutions in the country, with average entering SAT scores well above 1200 (based on the former possible score total of 1600), and both focused primarily on undergraduate education. Both were founded as men's colleges and have admitted female students for approximately 40 years. Although neither was extremely large, one campus was significantly larger than the other. The larger was approximately 7,000 students, including 1,600 graduate students, while the other enrolled 1,200 undergraduates.

Interviews at both institutions were conducted in the spring of 1999. All African American women who had started at either institution four years earlier and who were still enrolled were identified with the assistance of the administration and contacted for an interview. The institutions provided me with information from the students' Student Information Form surveys collected by the Cooperative Institutional Research Program (CIRP), sponsored by the Higher Education Research Institute (HERI) at UCLA and the American Council on Education (ACE). The 15 students who were contacted and interviewed from the larger institution, dubbed Traditional University (TU) for this study, were chosen with as much socioeconomic diversity as possible, using information from their freshman year surveys. All four African American women who started four years earlier at Small College (SC), the smaller institution, agreed to participate.

The students in this study, on the whole, came from middle- to upper-class families; only one student did not have a parent with some postsecondary experience (see Table 5.1). Thirteen of the students had at least one parent with a bachelor's degree, and 10 had at least one parent with a graduate

TABLE 5.1

Student Demographic Information

Student Name	SAT Math	SAT Verbal	Father's Education	Mother's Education	Family Income (in thousands)
Small College					
Clara	470	570	Grad degree	Voc/Tech	$75–99
Susan	410	630	Less than HS	Less than HS	$10–15
Rebecca	630	630	Grad degree	Some grad	$100–$150
Zelda	650	640	Grad degree	Grad degree	$100–$150
Traditional University					
LaSandra	620	610	Grammar sch.	Voc/Tech	$20–$25
Fatima	630	520	Bach. degree	Some college	$50–$60
Erin	570	570	HS	Grad degree	$40–$50
Nquita	670	510	Grad degree	Grad degree	$50–$60
Farrah	670	600	Grad degree	Grad degree	$60–$75
Kassandra	620	700	Grad degree	Grad degree	$75–$100
Daniella	710	650	Grad degree	Bach degree	$75–$100
Jasmine	570	550	Grad degree	Bach degree	$100–$150
Crystal	700	510	Some college	HS	$50–$60
Esmerelda	710	510	Some college	Voc/Tech	$30–$40
Aisha	690	610	Grad degree	Some college	$40–$50
Teresa	610	530	Grammar sch.	Some college	$20–$25
Kassie	700	570	Some college	Some college	$40–$50
Emma	710	570	Some grad	Some grad	$60–$75
Lynda	550	550	Bach degree	Bach degree	$100–$150

degree. Additionally, as is clear from Table 5.1, students had high SAT scores, and the majority came from middle- to upper-middle income families.

I personally conducted all interviews with students on the two campuses in a café or coffeehouse on campus over a two-month period. Each interview averaged between one hour and an hour and a half, was taped, and was transcribed verbatim. As a White woman, I was particularly conscious of establishing rapport. The rapport I was able to establish varied, but on the whole, I believe my rapport with the students was very good. I focused on building on commonalities as women and in the types of colleges attended, and other experiences, as seen in previous research (Horvat & Antonio, 1999). Rapport was evident in the students' warmth, including smiles, laughter, and occasional hugs at the end of the interviews. It was also evident in students' sharing of some of their most painful experiences, and their anger and tears in describing those experiences.

I asked students how they made decisions within the college environment regarding friends, major field, housing, and activities. I also asked them about their academic and social experiences as African Americans and as women on these campuses. I interviewed all of the students in the last few months before graduation, as they prepared to transition out of college and into graduate school or the workforce, and I asked them how they were making decisions about the future. I transcribed the interviews on an ongoing basis and coded them according to broad categories of emergent characteristics and activities consistent with a Bourdieuian framework, and categories, such as the role of campus social communities, that emerged from the data independent of the theoretical framework. Because of space constraints, I drew data for this study from students' social experiences, I reviewed them in an iterative process, consistent with grounded theory (Bogdan & Biklen, 2003), to develop an understanding of their experiences inductively. Patterns emerged that illustrated the effects of cultural capital and habitus in students' social experiences on campus and also illustrated the complex role African American campus communities played in those experiences on each campus.

Results and Discussion

Social activities are a primary focus for many college students. Yet, students in the study experienced significant conflict in the social realm, including isolation and rejection based on their race, social class, and gender. The two institutions differed in their social interaction and the effects of that interaction on the students I interviewed for this study. I discuss TU first, followed by SC.

Traditional University had a system of independent social houses that operated as quasi-fraternities and sororities. Many of these houses maintained connections with alumni, in part through alumni boards. Students became eligible to join in the spring of their sophomore year and, if they joined, students ate all their meals at the houses. If students did not join, they ate their meals in dining halls, mostly with freshmen and sophomores. The houses, though independent, operated with university sanction. The students' social activity revolved around parties, with heavy beer drinking and dancing to live music or DJs at the houses two nights a week. For students who did not attend these parties, there were few alternate social activities on campus.

These houses held very little appeal for many African American students, however, and eight of the students studied did not join a house. The houses were too expensive or seemed like a waste of money for these students, particularly because many of the students interviewed did not drink and knew that part of what they paid went to purchase beer. Additionally, the music was not music these students wanted to listen to, and their musical tastes, part of cultural capital, were not valued in the houses. Finally, the dating scene in the houses, which consisted of students drinking and participating in one-night stands, or "hooking up," was not appealing to these students. So the houses became sites where the African American students' economic capital was insufficient and where their values and tastes, their habitus and cultural capital, were explicitly dominated by White, upper-middle-class culture and values.

Jasmine told me: "I don't want to spend that much money on beer for a year. It's just not my style. It's not what I do on the weekends." Kassie said: "I couldn't afford it. It's really expensive . . . and I didn't drink." According to a third: "I don't drink . . . and they didn't play the music I would want to dance to." A fourth declared: "I don't listen to that type of music . . . [and] I'm just not into hooking up." "A meat market" is how yet another woman described the dating that took place. Nquita related an incident in which she and a friend asked a DJ who was taking requests during a party to play a song. The DJ told them "the [people] who hired us . . . told us exclusively no hip-hop music." She was very upset and told me, "So to me that was basically 'don't play any Black music in there.'"

Seven students did join, however, but six of them belonged for one year or less. They joined because friends joined, because the food was better, because they did not want to eat with underclassmen, and because they did want to participate in the social arena in some way. Erin said, "[The house] for me is basically a place to eat. . . . You're sort of separated from your classmates if [you] choose not to [join the houses]." Another said: "I heard they had the best food." Farrah was a vice president of one of the most exclusive houses. She recognized that the houses were exclusive and there were few other options for students, but saw the houses as part of the university culture. She told me, "The culture at [TU] is one of those things you can fight, but you gotta fight it really hard. And is it worth that much energy?"

Although the African American students I interviewed all had friends and, in many cases, good friends, for many, the overall social experience was one of isolation from the mainstream social networks on campus. Particularly given the access to social capital that house membership provided for current and former members, the African American students were often isolated and unable to accumulate the social capital that White students did. Their habitus, cultural capital, and economic capital marked them as different in the social scene at TU, and this difference resulted in African American students' accruing fewer of the benefits such a highly selective education provided to White students.

Overall, the SC students were less socially isolated than their TU counterparts. SC did not have the social houses, was smaller in size, and organized students into groups of 8 to 10 their first year. These groups functioned as pseudo families, and the African American women at SC socialized within these groups, particularly the first year or two. Clara said: "We had a very close-knit . . . group freshman year . . . you get to know people . . . the campus is so small, the student community is very small and . . . pretty close-knit." Susan "lived with three other people from my freshman year [group] . . . even this year." Zelda did not enjoy her freshman group because "these [people] had to be my brothers and sisters . . . I just didn't like being told who to like." Nonetheless, she found two friends freshman year and "then things just spiraled. I . . . met people they knew."

So, overall, the social patterns were quite different on these two campuses. However, on both campuses the African American women in this study felt different from their fellow students, felt marked by their class and racial differences. In describing their experiences on campus, many students mentioned the importance of race and socioeconomic status. One student said: "A lot of students . . . were oblivious to what it was . . . to not be White . . . the social life is . . . not like African American-friendly." Another TU student believed: "There are a lot of upper-class people and . . . they don't have a sense . . . they aren't sympathetic or understanding of what it's like to be in another class." She added: "A lot of times my friends and I joke . . . if I were White, this would be the best place." Yet another student saw herself as "different . . . I'm Black . . . this is a very WASPy school." At SC, Rebecca told me, she saw herself as "Black . . . in a very, very, very White place."

The effect of gender on the socialization process was remarkably similar on both campuses. One student who attended SC could have been talking about either university when she said, "In terms of dating . . . it's difficult for women . . . a lot of women . . . leave . . . with lower self-esteem." Interracial dating on both campuses was taboo, which several women found problematic. Characteristic of that sentiment, one told me: "Interracial dating . . . [is] a big taboo here . . . but where I grew up . . . you dated who you wanted to date." Other students saw dating as an issue because the African American communities were small and there were more women than men. One said: "One of the biggest problems . . . as African American women . . . there's more of us here than African American men." Yet another saw "the rise of a whole new set of bachelorette class." She and her friends "don't date . . . that's something that a lot of [my] . . . Black professional or educated female . . . friends [have in common], none of us . . . have anything like that on our . . . horizons. It's kind of depressing."

From these women's words, it was clear that, while they would like to have had companionship or a relationship, the dating scene on campus, with its "hookups," was unappealing, there were fewer African American men, and interracial dating was taboo for them as African American women. This left them even more isolated socially. In this context, what constituted an appropriate choice for a dating or relationship partner was unavailable. Their habitus was not congruent with the social realities on campus. Furthermore, discouraging interracial dating and marriage has also been documented as a value of middle- and upper-middle-class African Americans (Graham, 1999;

Pattillo-McCoy, 1999), so the campus taboos may reflect larger social values enforced through campus communities.

One method for coping with their sense of isolation was to join extracurricular activities. As previous research (Allen, 1992; Bennett, 1998) has found, many students became involved in clubs and groups that acknowledged and supported their ethnicity and gender. One student expressed what I heard from many others: "I found my clique with African Americans because [of] the activities I ended up being involved in." Regardless of the specific type of activity, student involvement is critical for students' change, growth, and retention, and these highly selective campuses foster involvement (Astin, 1993, 1999; Tinto, 1987). Most of the students in this study, with one exception, did become involved in some type of extracurricular or co-curricular activity, including ethnically or gender-based groups, university committees, campus publications, voluntary community groups, musical and theatrical groups, and sports teams. Those activities were shaped by the cultural capital students possessed and by their habitus. They chose their activities based on interest, but also on what they viewed as necessary and appropriate as African American women.

As African American women, many joined organizations focused specifically on them and their needs and culture. Organizations tied specifically to the African American community, such as sororities, Black student associations, or clubs for African American students with particular academic interests, were the activities mentioned most often, with 10 of the students discussing membership in such organizations during their interviews. The sororities these students joined were both race- and gender-specific. Four other students joined organizations specifically for women, which may well have provided haven and support in a sexist environment, as has been found in other research on women (Jackson, 1998). This was particularly true given the fact that the women's organizations students mentioned included organizations for women of color and women in nontraditional fields such as science and engineering. In addition to providing a haven in an isolating environment (Allen, 1992; Bennett, 1998), these organizations provide fictive kinship (Bennett, 1998), a type of extended family network important to middle-class African Americans (Conley, 1999; Pattillo-McCoy, 1999), as well as contacts and access to larger networks. These contacts constitute social capital that students may be able to convert in the future for social and occupational gain (LaMont & Lareau, 1988; Lareau, 1993; MacLeod, 1987;

McDonough et al., 1997). Previous research (Katchadourian & Boli, 1994; Zweigenhaft, 1993) has documented the importance of access to social capital in highly selective universities. Given that many of the students, particularly the TU students, felt socially isolated, these African American organizations seemed to provide access to alternative social capital that students will be able to use in the future.

Service organizations were very important activities for many students. Five students served as residential advisers responsible for advising and assisting their fellow students. Mentoring or tutoring was a popular activity, and most of this was aimed at local low-income and minority children. Seven women participated in some form of tutoring through campus-, community-, or sorority-sponsored groups. Five students reported participating in groups that built housing in the local communities, coordinated urban cleanups, and rehabilitated public spaces. Students gave similar reasons for involvement; they saw these groups as opportunities to "give back" to the communities. One told me she saw "a lot lacking in the educational system. And somehow I think that I can be like one of those people who can make a difference." Another who believed she "can give back to the community" was involved in a group that "did some renovating of houses . . . in [an] inner-city area." Contributing to the African American community, or giving back, is an important cultural value in middle- and upper-middle-class African American communities and is reflected in these students' choices. Religious groups and activities drew five members from the students as well, reflective of religion's cultural importance in the African American community (Graham, 1999; Pattillo-McCoy, 1999).

These activities were the ones that clearly resonated strongly with the students' values. These clubs and groups provided solace from isolation (Allen, 1992; Bennett, 1998) and were where students felt comfortable and at ease, important hallmarks of habitus (Bourdieu, 1977). They provided students with fictive kinship (Bennett, 1998), and previous work has documented the importance of extended family networks for middle-class African Americans. Such activities also offered service and religious experiences that scholars associate with middle- and upper-middle-class African American cultural values (Graham, 1999; Pattillo-McCoy, 1999). Moreover, these groups gave students the opportunity to build friendships, which constitute social capital students may find useful in the future (LaMont & Lareau, 1988; Lareau, 1993; MacLeod, 1987; McDonough et al., 1997). Yet, despite the importance of these culturally specific groups on campus and the solace they provided, many students saw tension within the African American community, and several students felt alienated and isolated from the African American campus community. Habitus was again the nexus of their alienation and isolation from the community.

Eight students spoke of being isolated or alienated from the African American community. It was an extremely painful topic for several of them to discuss. Some attributed it to social class; others, not feeling "Black enough," saw race as the cause. Often it was both race and class that separated these students. At SC, Rebecca explained that she "did grow up very White," and then spent freshman year "trying to figure out what it meant to be Black." She believed the African American community message to her was, "You're not Black enough." She felt "like I wasn't Black enough . . . I didn't dress Black. I didn't act Black. I didn't come from the right economic area or whatever it takes." She came from a fairly well-off family, saying, "I don't have to worry about money." Zelda told me: "I identify much more with the light [skinned] students . . . I think that's because of my class bracket . . . that's what makes it easier for me to be around White students." Susan, however, attributed her distance from the community to social class and had the opposite problem. There was a week when all minority students were invited to campus "and I was invited, but I could not afford to take a week off." When she arrived on campus, that group had "become closely bonded . . . it was already like a formed group. I didn't feel comfortable."

Common interests, or the lack of them, were another issue to which students attributed their lack of African American friends. Jasmine, who listens to National Public Radio (NPR), to classical music, and is a romance languages major, told me: "It's more than just skin color. I don't have a lot in common with them, and it's hard for me to be friends with them." Another TU student felt a "tension between . . . my interests . . . and what my race is . . . I just am into odd things like comic books and classical music, which is . . . classified as a White people's thing."

Much of the tension within the African American community seemed to revolve around issues of loyalty to that community and friendship patterns. Rebecca at SC said: "I used to get nasty looks in the cafeteria . . . because I didn't hang out [with African American students]." A TU student said, if "you hang out with too many non-Black people, then you kind of have a problem. . . . I ended up trying to have all kinds of friends and it just doesn't work that way. . . . I [got] . . . isolated from the Black community . . . I can't hang out with them." A third said: "If you're not sitting with all Black people, then you're kind of like a sellout . . . it's more within your own race [that] you have a problem." The last student quoted did not feel isolated, in part because most of her friends were African American. But she still believed the views of African Americans on campus to be problematical.

Other African Americans saw the same situation differently. Several students who did not speak of being isolated also mentioned the importance of socializing with African Americans and the isolation of those who did not. Kassie initially felt isolated at TU, and her strategy was: "Go find the minority kids and hang out with them." In a lengthy comment a student told me:

> I take the whole Black community here and . . . split it in half . . . [and one half are] people who don't really hang out with other Black people . . . I think there's something wrong with you if you have exclusively [White friends]. We call them people who don't associate. We just have this thing, if I see you on campus passing us and you're Black, I speak to you and you speak to me. It's just a given . . . and they [those who don't associate] won't speak . . . [it's] whacked.

Another student mentioned the same behavior of African Americans' "saying hi or whatever" when they met. She also saw people she called "incogs" or incognito, "who really just don't associate with the African American community at all . . . they avoid eye contact with you and just, like, don't speak ever." This kind of deeply ingrained, taken for granted behavior of acknowledging other African Americans is a cultural value and element of habitus, and many members of the community assume the African American students who violate this cultural norm do not want to associate with the Black community, an act often seen as disloyal.

So there was tension within the African American community as well as tension with being African American on a White campus. The tension within the community, for those who felt isolated, revolved around race, class, and taste in hobbies and music. These types of tastes, of course, are indicative of cultural capital, and the students who felt isolated believed the larger community did not value the African American students' cultural capital. The isolated students felt marked as different, and denied community membership, by their racial status, skin tone, and social class, that is by their habitus and, at times, their cultural capital. In contrast, the African American students who were part of the community on campus saw African Americans who were not members as violating a cultural norm of loyalty to the community in the form of friendship patterns with other African Americans and acknowledging other African American students in passing. Loyalty has been documented as part of middle- and upper-middle-class African American culture (Graham, 1999; Pattillo-McCoy, 1999), so the students' behavior on campus may reflect and enforce this particular habitus. Similar to earlier research on highly selective colleges and universities illustrating that particular elements of White upper-middle-class habitus and cultural capital were inculcated and reinforced (Domhoff, 1983; Kingston & Lewis, 1990; Useem & Karabel, 1986), the African American communities on these campuses may inculcate and reinforce the value of loyalty.

Conclusions and Implications

Clearly, students' social experiences on these two highly selective campuses were shaped by their habitus and cultural capital (Bourdieu, 1977, 1990, 1994). Their race, socioeconomic status, and gender all contributed to their habitus and cultural capital. That is, their tastes and preferences, the values they held, the situations in which they felt comfortable, and what they saw as possible and appropriate action were affected by their race, social class, and, to some extent, their gender. In general, students felt isolated, marginalized, and different from their White peers. Some students felt devalued within their own community as well as within the White community in general.

Scholars and practitioners have long acknowledged the role African American campus communities play in providing a haven for African American students in the often hostile environments of PWIs (Allen, 1992; Bennett, 1998), and the data clearly illustrate that role for the communities on these campuses. But this study suggests two additional roles of the African American community. The first is to provide African American students with social capital, or the friendships and contacts that may be converted in the future for occupational or social gain (LaMont & Lareau, 1988; Lareau, 1993; MacLeod, 1987; McDonough, et al., 1997). This is particularly important because many of these students experienced restricted access to social capital accumulation opportunities to which White students had access. The second role is to inculcate and reinforce middle- and upper-middle-class African American cultural values, including the importance of familial-like networks, religion, and service and loyalty to the community (Conley, 1999; Graham, 1999; Pattillo-McCoy, 1999). Previous research on highly selective campuses found that these institutions inculcate and reinforce upper-class values and social ties in White students who attend them (Domhoff, 1983; Katchadourian & Boli, 1994; Kingston & Lewis, 1990; Useem & Karabel, 1986; Zweigenhaft, 1993); however, the data in this study point to a similar role for the African American communities on these campuses.

There has been much research and angst in higher education regarding diversity and self-segregation on campuses (Bennett, 1998; Tatum, 1997); yet, this study suggests multiple roles for campus ethnic communities. This is significant because researchers have not explored the role of ethnic communities in inculcating values specific to the larger community, as has been found in highly selective PWIs (Domhoff, 1983; Katchadourian & Boli, 1994; Kingston & Lewis, 1990; Useem & Karabel, 1986; Zweigenhaft, 1993). Further research is needed to understand more fully the complexities of campus ethnic communities and their roles in different types of institutions.

Practitioners can also use the results of this study. First, they can focus on the campus social structures to ensure access to all students. These structures, particularly if student-led, can be very intractable; however, the isolation and marginalization these students experienced must be addressed and lessened. The study can also provide practitioners with new ways to view African American campus communities. Rather than worrying about self-segregation (Bennett, 1998; Tatum, 1997), practitioners can assist these communities in strengthening their alumni networks and recognizing their unique contributions.

This study highlights the importance of considering race, class, and gender in understanding students' college experiences. Researchers should work to understand how all three identity statuses work in concert to shape college students' experiences. Furthermore, more work needs to be done to highlight and address the needs of marginalized student groups. Our campuses must be welcoming for all students, and the benefits of the education we provide must extend to all groups. Research may provide important insights in these arenas.

References

Alexander-Snow, M. (1999). Two African American women graduates of historically White boarding schools and their social integration at a traditionally White university. *The Journal of Negro Education, 68*(1), 106–119.

Allen, W. R. (1988). The education of Black students on White college campuses: What quality the experience? In M. T. Nettles (Ed.), *Toward Black undergraduate student equality in American higher education* (pp. 57–85). Westport, CT: Greenwood Press.

Allen, W. R. (1991). Introduction. In W. R. Allen, E. G. Epps, & N. Z. Haniff (Eds.), *College in Black and White: African American students in predominantly White and in historically Black public universities* (pp. 1–14). Albany, NY: State University of New York Press.

Allen, W. (1992). The color of success: African American college student outcomes at predominantly White and historically Black public colleges and universities. *Harvard Educational Review, 62*(1), 26–44.

Allen, W. R., & Haniff, N. Z. (1991). Race, gender and academic performance in U.S. higher education. In W. R. Allen, E. G. Epps, & N. Z. Haniff (Eds.), *College in Black and White: African American students in predominantly White and in historically Black public universities* (pp. 95–109). Albany, NY: State University of New York Press.

Astin, A. W. (1993). *What matters in college? Four critical years revisited.* San Francisco, CA: Jossey-Bass.

Astin, A. W. (1999). How the liberal arts college affects students. *Daedalus, 128*(1), 77–100.

Bennett, S. M. (1998). Self-segregation: An oxymoron in Black and White. In K. Freeman (Ed.), *African American culture and heritage in higher education research and practice* (pp. 121–132). Westport, CT: Praeger Press.

Bogdan, R., & Biklen, S. (2003). *Qualitative research for education* (4th ed.). Boston, MA: Allyn and Bacon.

Bourdieu, P. (1977). Cultural reproduction and social reproduction. In J. Karabel & A. H. Halsey (Eds.), *Power and ideology in education* (pp. 487–511). New York: Oxford University Press.

Bourdieu, P. (1990). Artistic taste and cultural capital. In J. Alexander and S. Seidman, (Eds.), *Culture and society: Contemporary debates* (pp. 205–215). Cambridge, MA: Cambridge University Press.

Bourdieu, P. (1994). Distinction: A social critique. In D. B. Grusky (Ed.), *Social stratification: Class, race, and gender in sociological perspective* (pp. 404–429). Boulder, CO: Westview Press.

Bowen, W., & Bok, D. (1998). *The shape of the river*. Princeton, NJ: Princeton University Press.

Braddock, J. H., & McPartland, J. M. (1988). Some cost and benefit considerations for Black college students attending predominately White versus predominately Black universities. In M. T. Nettles (Ed.), *Toward Black undergraduate student equality in American higher education* (pp. 87–104). Westport, CT: Greenwood Press.

Cabrera, A. F., Nora, A., & Terenzini, P. T. (1999). Campus racial climate and the adjustment of students to college: A comparison between White students and African American students. *The Journal of Higher Education, 70*(2), 134–160.

Carter, D. J., & Wilson, R. (1996). *Minorities in higher education*. Washington, DC: American Council on Education.

Cary, L. (1991). *Black ice*. New York: Vintage Books.

Conley, D. (1999). *Being Black, living in the red: Race, wealth, and social policy in America*. Berkeley, CA: University of California Press.

D'Augelli, A. R., & Hershberger, S. L. (1993). African American undergraduates on a predominantly White campus: Academic factors, social networks, and campus climate. *Journal of Negro Education, 62*(1), 67–81.

Davis, J. E. (1998). Cultural capital and the role of historically Black colleges and universities in educational reproduction. In K. Freeman (Ed.), *African American culture and heritage in higher education research and practice* (pp. 143–154). Westport, CT: Praeger Press.

Davis, M., Dias-Bowie, Y., Greenberg, K., Klukken, G., Pollio, H., Thomas, S., & Thompson, C. (2004). "A fly in the buttermilk": Descriptions of university life by successful Black undergraduate students at a predominantly White southeastern university. *The Journal of Higher Education, 75*(4), 420–445.

Davis, R. B. (1991). Social support networks and undergraduate student academic-success-related outcomes: A comparison of Black students on Black and White campuses. In W. R. Allen, E. G. Epps, & N. Z. Haniff (Eds.), *College in Black and White: African American students in predominantly White and in historically Black public universities* (pp. 143–157). Albany, NY: State University of New York Press.

DiMaggio, P., & Mohr, J. (1985). Cultural capital, educational attainment, and marital selection. *American Journal of Sociology, 90*(6), 1231–1261.

Domhoff, G. W. (1983). *Who rules America now?* New York: Simon & Schuster.

Fleming, J. (1984). *Blacks in college*. San Francisco, CA: Jossey-Bass.

Freeman, K. (1997). Increasing African Americans' participation in higher education: African American high-school students' perspectives. *The Journal of Higher Education, 68*, 523–550.

Freeman, K. (1999). The race factor in African Americans' college choice. *Urban Education, 34*(1), 4–25.

Graham, L. O. (1995). *Member of the club: Reflections on life in a racially polarized world.* New York: HarperPerennial.

Graham, L. O. (1999). *Our kind of people: Inside America's Black upper class.* New York: HarperPerennial.

Hamilton, C. W. (1996). Nature of motivation for educational achievement among African American female college students. *Urban Education, 31*(1), 72–90.

Haniff, N. Z. (1991). Epilogue. In W. R. Allen, E. G. Epps, & N. Z. Haniff (Eds.), *College in Black and White: African American students in predominantly White and in historically Black public universities* (pp. 247–256). Albany, NY: State University of New York Press.

Hoffnung, R. J., & Sack, A. L. (1981). *Does higher education reduce or reproduce social class differences? Schooling at Yale University, University of Connecticut, and University of New Haven, and student attitudes and expectations regarding future work.* Paper presented at the Annual Meeting of the Eastern Psychological Association, New York, NY.

Horvat, E. M. (2000). Understanding equity and access in higher education: The potential contribution of Pierre Bourdieu. In J. C. Smart & W. Tierney (Eds.), *The higher education handbook of theory and research* (Vol. 16, pp. 195–238). Hingham, MA: Kluwer Academic Publishers.

Horvat, E. M., & Antonio, A. L. (1999). "Hey, those shoes are out of uniform": African American girls in an elite high school and the importance of habitus. *Anthropology & Education Quarterly, 30*(3), 317–342.

Jackson, K. W., & Swan, L. A. (1991). Institutional and individual factors affecting Black undergraduate student performance: Campus race and student gender. In W. R. Allen, E. G. Epps, & N. Z. Haniff (Eds.), *College in Black and White: African American students in predominantly White and in historically Black public universities* (pp. 127–141). Albany, NY: State University of New York Press.

Jackson, L. R. (1998) The influence of both race and gender on the experiences of African American college women. *The Review of Higher Education, 21*(4), 359–375.

Karabel, J. (1972). Community colleges and social stratification. *Harvard Educational Review, 42*(4), 521–562.

Karabel, J., & Astin, A. W. (1975). Social class, academic ability, and college quality. *Social Forces, 53*(3), 381–398.

Katchadourian, H., & Boli, J. (1994). *Cream of the crop: The impact of elite education in the decade after college.* New York: Basic Books.

Kingston, P. W., & Lewis, L. S. (1990). Introduction: Studying elite schools in America. In P. W. Kingston & L. S. Lewis (Eds.), *The high status track: Studies of elite schools and stratification* (pp. xi–xxxiv). Albany, NY: State University of New York Press.

Kingston, P. W., & Smart, J. C. (1990). The economic pay-off of prestigious colleges. In P. W. Kingston & L. S. Lewis (Eds.), *The high status track: Studies of elite schools and stratification* (pp. 147–174). Albany, NY: State University of New York Press.

LaMont, M., & Lareau, A. (1988). Cultural capital: Allusions, gaps, and glissandos in recent theoretical developments. *Sociological Theory, 6,* 153–168.

Lareau, A. (1993). *Home advantage: Social class and parental intervention in elementary education.* Philadelphia, PA: The Falmer Press.

MacKay, K. A., & Kuh, G. D. (1994). A comparison of student effort and educational gains of Caucasian and African American students at predominantly White colleges and universities. *Journal of College Student Development, 35,* 217–223.

MacLeod, J. (1987). *Ain't no makin' it: The leveled aspirations of a low-income neighborhood.* Boulder, CO: Westview Press.

Matthews, W., & Jackson, K. W. (1991). Determinants of success for Black males and females in graduate and professional schools. In W. R. Allen, E. G. Epps, & N. Z. Haniff (Eds.), *College in Black and White: African American students in predominantly White and in historically Black public universities* (pp. 197–208). Albany, NY: State University of New York Press.

McDonough, P. M. (1997). *Choosing colleges: How social class and schools structure opportunity.* Albany, NY: State University of New York Press.

McDonough, P. M., Antonio, A., & Trent, J. (1997). Black students, Black colleges: An African American college-choice model. *Journal for a Just and Caring Education, 3,* 9–36.

Nettles, M. T. (1991). Racial similarities and differences in the predictors of college student achievement. In W. R. Allen, E. G. Epps, & N. Z. Haniff (Eds.), *College in Black and White: African American students in predominantly White and in historically Black public universities* (pp. 75–91). Albany, NY: State University of New York Press.

Pascarella, E., & Terenzini, P. T. (2005). *How college affects students: A third decade of research* (Vol. 2). San Francisco, CA: Jossey-Bass.

Patillo-McCoy, M. (1999). *Black picket fences: Privilege and peril among the Black middle class.* Chicago, IL: University of Chicago Press.

Solmon, L. (1975). The definition of college quality and its impact on earnings. *National Bureau of Economic Research, 2,* 537–587.

Tatum, B. D. (1997). *"Why are all the Black kids sitting together in the cafeteria?" and other conversations about race.* New York: Basic Books.

Taylor, R., & Olswang, S. (1997). Crossing the color line: African Americans and predominantly White universities. *College Student Journal, 31*(1), 11–20.

Thompson, C., & Fretz, B. (1991). Predicting the adjustment of Black students at predominantly White institutions. *Journal of Higher Education, 62*(4), 437–450.

Tinto, V. (1987). *Leaving college.* Chicago, IL: University of Chicago Press.

U.S. Department of Education, National Center for Education Statistics (NCES). (2005). *Digest of education statistics.* Available online at http://nces.ed.gov/

Useem, M., & Karabel, J. (1986). Pathways to top corporate management. *American Sociological Review, 51,* 184–200.

Walpole, M., McDonough, P. M., Bauer, C. J., Gibson, C., Kanyi, K., & Toliver, R. (2005). This test is unfair: Urban African American and Latino high school students' perceptions of standardized college admission tests. *Urban Education, 40*(3) 321–349.

West, C. (1994). *Race matters.* Boston: Beacon Press.

White, L. S. (1998). "Am I Black enuf fo ya?" Black student diversity: Issues of identity and community. In K. Freeman (Ed.), *African American culture and heritage in higher education research and practice* (pp. 93–120). Westport, CT: Praeger Press.

Wilson, R. (1998). African American participation in higher education. In K. Freeman (Ed.), *African American culture and heritage in higher education research and practice* (pp. 7–12). Westport, CT: Praeger Press.

Wilson, W. J. (1980). *The declining significance of race: Blacks and changing American institutions.* Chicago, IL: University of Chicago Press.

Zweigenhaft, R. (1993). Prep school and public school graduates of Harvard: A longitudinal study of the accumulation of social and cultural capital. *Journal of Higher Education, 64,* 211–225.

PART THREE

THE GRADUATE EXPERIENCE

6

PROFESSIONAL SOCIALIZATION, POLITICIZED RACED AND GENDERED EXPERIENCE, AND BLACK FEMALE GRADUATE STUDENTS

A Roadmap for Structural Transformation

Venice Thandi Sulé

The struggle to end domination, the individual struggle to resist colonization, to move from object to subject, is expressed in the effort to establish the liberatory voice—the way of speaking that is no longer determined by one's status as object—as oppressed being. That way of speaking is characterized by opposition, by resistance.

(hooks, 1989, p. 15)

Historically, Black female access to America's most influential research institutions was systemically obstructed (Evans, 2007; Giddings, 1984).[1] However, in the wake of resistance movements and international embarrassment, legislative action was taken to eradicate barriers to education and employment attainment (D. Bell, 1995, 2004). As a result, African American women, like their male counterparts, gained access to predominantly White [higher-education] institutions (PWIs) (W. Allen et al., 2002; Glazer-Raymo, 1999; Trower, 2002; Trower & Chait,

2002). However, once enrolled they encountered gendered and racialized conditions that hindered their ability to navigate these institutions (Thomas & Hollenshead, 2001; Turner & Myers, 2000; Turner & Thompson, 1993). Their marginalization continues and is a testament to the pervasiveness of race and gender subjugation and the normalization of hierarchical power structures.

The conditions that marginalize African American students within PWIs are embedded within the professional socialization process. Professional socialization is essentially the process by which individuals are groomed to uphold organizational norms (Dunn, Rouse, & Seff, 1994; Tierney & Rhoads, 1993). Fundamentally, it entails learning and employing the cultural perspective of the workplace (Van-Maanen & Schein, 1979). In this vein, professional socialization is a mode of cultural transference consisting of a "ritualized process that involves the transmission of culture" (Tierney & Rhoads, 1993, p. 21). Professional socialization has also been acknowledged as a gender biased process that disadvantages women because the norms are designed to meet the needs of males (Tierney & Bensimon, 1996; Ward & Bensimon, 2002). Essentially, academe promulgates cultural practices "that not only institutionalize gender inequities but also induce women to act out stereotypical female roles to gain acceptance by their predominately White male senior colleagues" (Ward & Bensimon, 2002, p. 431). Similarly, it can be reasoned that academic professional socialization is also "raced" because it supports and reinforces institutional racism.[2] In short, the attitudes, values, and skills that comprise professional socialization are neither gender nor race neutral, but instead are mirrors of hegemonic practices found within the larger social order.

History reveals that Black females have challenged hegemonic practices and discourses that impeded development within the Black community (Davis, 1981; Giddings, 1984; Hine & Thompson, 1998). As such, raced and gendered hierarchical power structures acted as catalysts for insurgency. In their enactments of resistance, Black women embodied oppositional positions, an awareness of being members of a socially marginalized group combined with behavioral and attitudinal resistance to individual and collective marginalization (Sulé, 2008). This chapter examines the professional socialization experiences of Black female graduate students that complicate achievement because majority (White and male) privilege is upheld in the production and transmission of knowledge. Additionally, this chapter looks at how race and gender barriers can act as springboards for institutional transformation.

Black Women in Higher Education

The literature on the professional socialization of Black female graduate students is virtually nonexistent. Thus, I surveyed a range of research on the Black female experience in academe from the undergraduate experience through the professoriate. Though these studies used students or professors as units of analysis, collectively they revealed factors that impede and facilitate negotiation of the academy.

Studies examining the intersection of race and gender at the undergraduate level suggest that Black females in PWIs encounter structural constraints complicated by their identity (Alfred, 2001; B. J. Allen, 1995; Constantine & Watt, 2002; Jackson, 1998; Myers, 2002; O'Connor, 2002; Thomas, 2001; Woods, 2001). For instance, O'Connor (2002) found that Black female undergraduates dealt with varying degrees of discriminatory behaviors from faculty and fellow students. In a comparative study of Black female experiences at historically Black and historically White institutions, Constantine and Watt (2002) found that participants at the PWIs had lower cultural congruity (fit between personal values and institutional values) and life satisfaction ratings than students attending Black institutions.

Themes of alienation and racial hostility continue among Black female graduate students and faculty. In Ellis's (2001) study, Black female graduate students viewed their experiences differently than Black male and White female graduate students. These women felt more isolated and less satisfied with their departments. Other studies found that Black female graduate students and faculty felt intellectually devalued and hindered from developing professionally (Alfred, 2001; B. J. Allen, 1995; Gregory, 1999; Holmes, 2001; Myers, 2002; Thomas & Hollenshead, 2001; Turner & Thompson, 1993; Woods, 2001). As a result, they had limited access to networking opportunities that promote career advancement. Some researchers contend that women who lack apprenticeship are at risk for accumulative disadvantages that occur when initial disadvantages, such as lack of mentoring, mushroom and limit career options and opportunities (Clark & Corcoran, 1986).

While these challenges have their debilitating effects, there is research to suggest that marginality enhances tenacity, thereby promoting resilience.

Alfred (2001), for example, found that tenured Black female faculty believed that their marginal status was an asset. Her participants employed what she termed "creative marginalization," the ability to view marginality from a perspective of difference rather than inferiority. In essence, their marginality required that they become culturally competent in different social arenas, thereby giving them the skills needed to work in various social contexts. Creative marginalization calls to mind the dialectical relationship between oppression and resistance. Black women have historically defied institutional and interpersonal subjugation by employing tactics that foster successful navigation between Black and White communities (Hill Collins, 2000). Their ability to occupy oppositional spaces was a testament to their ingenuity and their contribution to Black community survival. Furthermore, their capacity to maneuver between dominant and marginalized spaces provided insider knowledge about how hierarchical power relationships undermine Black advancement. As a result, Black women used this knowledge to advocate for social equity.

The literature reveals a long-standing tension between Black women and the academy that ultimately influences professional socialization. Again, inherent in the notion of professional socialization is internalizing and enacting the cultural perspective of an organization. However, as in the case of Black women, employing the cultural perspective of the workplace can be tantamount to self-negation because that perspective may devalue one's lived experiences. In response to the way professional socialization impedes full access into academe, Black women have used their marginal location as a space for empowerment. For instance, drawing from knowledge of dominant group norms and their social location, Black women have contemplated the multitude of factors that contribute to their condition and have acted in ways that promote transcendence of barriers. For these reasons, the dialectic between social position and resistance serves as the basis for the theoretical approaches used in this study.

Theoretical Foundation

The theories supporting this study are Black Feminist Thought and Political Race. Together, these theoretical frames map how social identities of race and gender intersect to influence access to professional socialization resources. The first theory, Black Feminist Thought (BFT), is premised upon the idea that the coupling of race and gender gives Black women a distinct and subordinate social location. This distinct location fosters common experiences and responses to the social structure, which form the basis of Black women's standpoints—a form of knowledge that challenges normative discourses about social conditions (Hill Collins, 2000; King, 1995). By acknowledging Black women as a unit of analysis, BFT provides a means for naming privileges and disadvantages accumulated through this particular group membership.

The second theoretical frame, Political Race, is used to associate race with a political identity, because race is linked to power. Political race postulates race as a mechanism used by power elites to justify and normalize power hierarchies (Guinier & Torres, 2002). The concept of political race is most useful to this study because, as a corollary, it embodies the idea that racialized groups function as barometers of social injustice. In other words, because oppressed groups are most vulnerable to structural constraints, they warn us of toxins in the social environment. Given their roles in sensitizing society about structural perils, racially subjugated groups also act as the catalysts for and directors of transformative social action (Guinier & Torres, 2002). Political race is an important social justice concept because it offers a method of analyzing power relations and tool for promoting institutional transformation.

Together BFT and Political Race help explain why it is important to look at the professional socialization experiences of a socially marginalized group. The raced and gendered experiences of Black female graduate students can act as warning signs to dysfunctional aspects of PWIs. These dysfunctions manifest as practices that systematically disadvantage Black women (and other groups) in order to maintain the epistemological and representational dominance of White males. Therefore, anything that challenges the dominant paradigm of scholarship (e.g., positivistic, quantitative, accessible only to scholars, and derived from socially dominant standpoints) and/or a scholar (i.e., White and male) is viewed with suspicion. However, what begins as a way to undermine the legitimacy of marginalized groups becomes a way to stifle the contributions of everyone. As Guinier and Torres (2002) explain, the inequities faced by one marginalized group can lead to awareness of interconnected inequities that affect other groups. In addition, the experiences of Black women inform institutions of how to be more inclusive so that the talents and perspectives of a diverse community are reflected throughout the academic environment.

Methods

The study sought to discover the essential meanings that the respondents applied to their experiences as Black female graduate students (Creswell, 1998; Strauss & Corbin, 1998; Weiss, 1994). To do so, I used theoretical sampling techniques (Creswell, 1998) to recruit 12 Black female graduate students (master's and doctoral level) with at least 1 year of coursework from a public research university. Among the participants, 4 were in science and engineering fields and 8 were in social science disciplines. Using a semi-structured protocol, I interviewed the participants for approximately 2 hours about the following concerns: (a) family and education background, (b) higher education experiences, and (c) engagement with the Black community. For this study, I focused on higher education experiences.

The use of comparative interpretation methods defined emerging themes. After employing local integration techniques (Weiss, 1994), the summarization of interviews by focusing on what is articulated and what I think it means, I used open coding to identify categories and their dimensions. The language of the participants guided the development of the coding process. Once the initial codes were developed, they were compared and contrasted to bring forth more complex and inclusive categories (Strauss & Corbin, 1998). Moreover, to enhance validity of the outcomes, the themes were referenced back to the participants' narratives to ensure close alignment with the interpretative outcome. Member checks were also conducted. To assist in transferability (the ability for other researchers to make inferences about a similar population based on this study), contextual information is provided (Guba & Lincoln, 1982).

Finally, this work acknowledges that meaning is co-constructed, the co-authoring of meaning through human interaction (Heyl, 2001; Taylor, 2001). It is a reflection of the principle of reflexivity, which asserts that it is impossible for me as the researcher to be objective and separate from the research. Therefore, I am aware of my influence on the construction of knowledge presented in this chapter. As an African American female with a PhD from a PWI, I come with intimate knowledge of the issue in question. The data is situated because factors such as participant identity, level of familiarity, and self-interest may determine what information participants share with me. Reflexively, I desire to understand how race and gender matter in my professional socialization process.

According to BFT, my social identity is an asset for this form of research. Black female scholars are encouraged to rearticulate the taken-for-granted knowledge of Black women as a means to challenge hegemony and to awaken the critical consciousness of Black women (Hill Collins, 2000). Accordingly, Black female scholars who use BFT as a theoretical framework are furthering the empowerment of Black women as: (a) Black women have critical insights based on personal experiences, (b) Black female scholars are not as likely to abandon BFT research when it is not expedient, (c) Black female scholars are needed to articulate Black female self-definition because empowerment is derived from self-authorship, and (d) Black female scholars are needed to help forge coalitions among Black women and other groups as a means to enhance consciousness about subjugated experiences (Hill Collins, 2000). Therefore, my identity is a constructive resource for data collection and analysis in the present study.

Findings

Participants

All except one participant grew up in two-parent, self-described middle-class households. Most stated that their parents had high educational expectations and structured their lives to ensure that they received a good education. Also, three of the four science and engineering students participated in pipeline science and engineering summer programs. In all, their experiences support the research that shows a relationship between parental education, social class, and college access (Cabrera & Nasa, 2000; Pascarella & Terenzini, 1991). Most notably, the women shared a multigenerational appreciation for education within their families, attesting to the historical high regard that Blacks have for education (Anderson, 1988; Giddings, 1984).

The advantages of familial educational experience and engagement notwithstanding, each of the participants found aspects of their learning environment hostile to their intersected race and gender identities. This analysis focuses on hostile raced and gendered professional socialization experiences of the participants and how those very experiences inspire resistance that may foster a commitment to social justice.

Race and Gender Hostility in Graduate School

Rather than overt forms of discrimination, participants discussed subtle yet ever-present incidents of bias or micro-aggressions. Micro-aggressions are subtle verbal or nonverbal acts of disregard that emanate from beliefs about the inferiority of targeted groups (Solorzano & Ceja, 2000). It is not a singular micro-aggressive act that is debilitating. What makes micro-aggressions insidious is that they are pervasive and difficult to define individually, yet collectively they amass a significant negative weight. For instance, Angela stated:

> It's so subtle in this school. You can't point to anything yet you know it exists. How about if you go to office hours by yourself, you typically don't get as much help as when you go with a group of students. Or how about when I go to office hours and I leave unclear and another student can go to office hours with very distinct answers to questions. Why? Everything is so subtle. Nobody would ever say you don't belong here or I'm not going to help you, but they help you very little or your questions aren't answered very well and you begin to think I must be asking the dumbest questions in the whole world. I can't say I've experienced any overt bias but I also know the bias in this school runs deep and you feel it and yet you can't put your finger on it.

Congruent with contemporary expressions of racism, most of these women's experiences with racism were subtle. In other words, policies and practices were not explicitly implemented to discriminate against Black women. Krysan (2000) calls this type of racism *new racism* because it reflects discordance between White egalitarian beliefs and White opposition to egalitarian practices when there is a perceived threat to one's social status. This type of racism is particularly insidious because it is typically cloaked within discussions of fairness, merit, individualism, and cultural norms (J. Dovidio, 1997; J. F. Dovidio & Gaertner, 1998; Eberhardt & Fiske, 1998; Krysan, 2000). Therefore, those on the receiving end of racism are often blamed for their inability to conform or are not given opportunities to excel because of perceived deficits.

Most of the participants did not speak about gender issues explicitly when describing challenges in their professional socialization process. This could be because gender was not perceived to be a major factor in how they navigated their institutions. Another explanation is that race subordinates gender in ways that make it a key determinant in how many Black females interpret their experiences (Higginbotham, 1992). Higginbotham explains:

> By continually expressing overt and covert analogic [*sic*] relationships, race impregnates the simplest meanings we take for granted. It makes hair "good" or "bad," speech patterns "correct or "incorrect." It is in fact, the apparent overdeterminacy of race in Western culture, and particularly in the United States, that has permitted it to function as a metalanguage in its discursive representation and construction of social relations. (p. 255)

Given the manner in which race often influences how gender is experienced, many Black women readily identify primarily as racial beings. However, the participants in science and engineering were more likely to discuss gender as a marginalization factor. This may be due to the stark underrepresentation of women in the sciences (Huang, Taddese, & Walter, 2000; Rosser, 2004).

The hostility experienced by the women fall into three categories: (a) epistemological racism, (b) lack of intellectual support from faculty and peers, and (c) tokenism. These categories are not mutually exclusive and subthemes are embedded within larger themes. However, I have attempted to capture the most salient juxtapositions of race and power.

Epistemological Racism

Epistemological racism is the privileging of knowledge produced by and about dominant racial groups and denigrating knowledge produced by and about marginalized racial groups, particularly when it challenges the dominant discourse (Villalpando & Bernal, 2002). Hill Collins (2000) finds that the U.S. knowledge validation process is designed to protect the interest of elite White men. Therefore, scholars who claim new knowledge must "convince a scholarly community controlled by elite . . . avowedly heterosexual White men" (p. 253). The following narrative illustrates how nontraditional scholarship is discouraged as part of students' professional socialization process. MeMe shared how a highly regarded faculty advisor responded to her desire to study race and gender:

> I tell him that I'm interested in studying the effects of race and gender in organizations. He looks at me and he says, 'no one in the academy will be

interested in that. But people outside of the academy might be interested in that.' Then I've had people tell me that I should be careful studying issues of race and gender because you are a Black woman and that's just one more strike against you.

Epistemological racism extends beyond discouraging certain types of research. It also reflects how institutions uphold and transmit disparaging information about people of color. For instance, Bett explained that colleagues and faculty rely upon deficiency models to interpret Black experiences:

> Bias is really seen in the literature and research that the people around me are conducting where African Americans are always "at risk" . . . bias almost functions like unspoken racism within academia. No one talks about it, but it is seen through your research.

In all, epistemological racism is just a reminder that students may be steered away from research that questions the relationship between power and privilege. Furthermore, they may be directed toward research that affirms the interests of dominant groups. What underlies these practices is the notion that subjugated groups cannot make independent scholarly (and therefore worthy) contributions. If anything, their role is to support and reproduce traditional modes of scholarship.

Lack of Faculty and Peer Intellectual Support

One of the major expectations of graduate students is that they demonstrate mastery of a particular area of study. Doctoral students, in particular, are expected to articulate an area of study and engage in research that contributes to a body of knowledge as part of their professional socialization. How well students are able to negotiate these expectations may influence their success in their respective programs. A major component of this success is dependent upon mentoring from faculty. Lack of faculty support was overwhelmingly discussed by participants in science and engineering. For example, Angela described how the fellowship she felt during the recruitment period quickly dissipated once she matriculated:

> They had orientation. They had this recruiting weekend for minority students. . . . They sell you this whole song and dance about how supportive

the institution is and how wonderful the professors are. While I'd admit that the professors at [the University] are brilliant, but they are not about teaching. You learn that pretty quickly. If you have deficiencies . . . the answers are usually like you got here so you should have known something. It's not the encouragement of if you work hard enough and I kind of direct you. It was a very tough living experience all around. After about the middle of my second semester, I was like if I graduate with my masters, I'll be good enough to leave here and I'll be happy . . . which is never the attitude that I had before. [The University] was like living hell . . . I have this attitude. If I know where to learn it, I am capable of learning anything.

Angela also was surprised by the lack of camaraderie among students. She explained that peers often refused to reciprocate help with coursework:

Even though I grew up in a competitive environment, the competition here is different. The competitive school environment I grew up in, we helped each other. I'm not used to the backstabbing people asking me questions just to see what I know . . . I was always willing and sharing, then I realized if I don't understand something those same people aren't necessarily going to help me. That was a very hard learning experience for me.

Angela's experience demonstrates how lack of peer intellectual support can heighten feelings of isolation. Similarly, Kendra expressed that students from historically Black colleges and universities (HBCUs) are automatically deemed deficient and are treated with less respect:

A statement has been said my first year here by a professor and it basically said that you don't belong here. You're not prepared to do the work. I took that and I guess it motivated me more. Every time I saw him after that I would make a point to say hello and let him know that I'm still here.

Kendra's narrative is an example of how the concept of Blackness is often believed to undermine the notion of merit, and also illustrates her resistance to the faculty member's belief regarding her merit. As a result, Blackness (Black people and Black schools) is viewed with suspicion.

Amerie's account adds to this picture of moving through spaces tinged with racial hostility. Here, she described how other students reacted to a large cohort of students of color:

> It was so stark my first couple years . . . because we were a large cohort of students of color. There were like six or seven of us . . . and so, people I think were just freaked out. We had to take these math and stats courses, and we were all struggling. The White kids . . . didn't want to work with us . . . I think they just automatically assumed that we couldn't really contribute . . . I don't know if they were like, "oh well they're dumb Black kids," but you know I felt like implicitly it was like "we don't need to work with you because you have nothing to contribute."

She felt that her peers took their cues from faculty. She described the classroom as a breeding ground for racial hostility:

> I think some of their impressions of us were shaped by how the faculty treated us. I had one stats class where the professor . . . had to say to the minority students that "you're not getting any special treatment." Yes, he pointed that out to us, plain as day . . . he was trying to put it in the context that I treat all my students equally. But that's just very insulting because you don't need to say that to me. I don't expect anything from you. But he did say you're not getting any special treatment . . . in statistics we had a TA who was a complete asshole . . . he had told other students . . . that we were just like Affirmative Action data and we didn't need to be here . . . we didn't find this out until later, but we all noticed that he was not pleasant to us, and he failed all of us in stats.

Amerie explained that the climate was so bad that the Black students had to take their concerns to the graduate school. The department eventually had to "really fix the situation." Altogether, these narratives show that race did factor into how peers and faculty responded to the participants.

Tokenism

Overwhelmingly, the lack of proportional representation of Blacks and women influenced how the participants were able to function in their departments. Kanter (1977) states that a marked imbalance (less than 15% of the total group) in representation results in tokenism—a state in which underrepresented groups are less integrated into organizations. As a result, underrepresented groups experience heightened performance pressures and are expected to play caricatured roles based on stereotypes. Belinda discussed how her race and gender placed her in a precarious situation:

Being a Black female makes it difficult when you're in group situations in science because they are not comfortable with women and they have no idea about Black people . . . I can't even say that they know what they're doing. They have a tendency to want to control everything. If you are in a lab, they want to do everything. And you are like, I need this experience just as much as you do.

Belinda had to negotiate the negative attitudes toward women and the ignorance that prompts stereotypical views about Black people and had to resist this aspect of professional socialization. In this case as in many others, the lack of diversity in the sciences combined with the normalization of White and gender privileges renders the intersection of Blackness and femaleness a disadvantage. Dorothy's account of her initial impression of the student population echoes the portrayal given by Belinda. Though she attended predominantly White primary and secondary schools, she felt intimidated by the lack of Blacks in her graduate classes:

Honestly, I did feel uncomfortable for a while going into those classrooms. I stepped into the room . . . and it was very, very shocking for me. Maybe it's the fact that grad students in general don't talk to each other . . . So it's like not only am I the only one or one of the few, I don't even know these people and no one is talking to anybody. So, it's not even like I can feel comfortable with you. It's like *double uncomfortable* because I don't know you and I'm different from you.

In attempting to find the words to explain her experience, Dorothy selected the phrase "double uncomfortable" to signify how her identity intersected with her perception of the climate. Her choice of words is reminiscent of how others have described the experiences of Black women in White institutions (E. E. Bell & Nkomo, 2001; Hill Collins, 2000; Hine, 1995; McKay, 2002). For instance, Bell and Nkomo contend that Black women are "double tokens" within corporate settings because they are extremely underrepresented. Correspondingly, McKay (2002) wrote that Black women in PWIs "experience the workplace as one of society's exclusive clubs to which, even though they have as much right as everyone else to be there, they will never gain full membership" (p. 21).

These accounts of tokenism signify lack of acceptance despite structural access into graduate programs. The African American women's formal membership in a high status group is offset by membership in a marginalized (or raced and gendered) group. Anna's narrative most poignantly reflects this marginalization in the classroom environment:

> I was in a class and we are talking about issues of class and race in the university environment and I came into the classroom late. It's obvious that . . . I'm frustrated. I try to buy into the conversation which I probably shouldn't have done but I start to make some comments along those lines. I used a very current experience. One of my girlfriend's electricity was cut off and it was the dead of winter. I was so late for class because there were like ten of us in the house trying to use one restroom . . . I shared that and I was told that that was inappropriate. My thinking is how is that inappropriate? It's very much germane to the issue. Is it inappropriate because it affects your comfort level? Because it's getting a little too close to home now, that you know somebody whose electricity is off . . . or their water's off and I discovered that the person was the biggest hypocrite because how are you going to stand there and try to lecture me about sensitivity and multiculturalism and Affirmative Action, and I am sitting here telling you what the experience is and you don't hear it. It's not germane. Just to think about it makes me angry.

Not only was Anna ignored but she was also silenced. Her attempts to contribute to a conversation about social equity by calling upon her experience were invalidated. The fact that Anna's experience was deemed inappropriate is an example of the epistemological difference between Black women and the larger society. Black feminist epistemology, unlike the dominant positivist approaches in research institutions, does not require physical and emotional distance (Hill Collins, 2000). People are not divorced from social structure. Experience and history matter. In essence, Anna believed that sharing her experience was a valid way to inform the theoretical discussion, yet that belief was a form of resistance to the dominant positivist approach that informed her professional socialization.

Summary

The narratives show that the participants were isolated and silenced within their graduate programs. Many of their problems resulted from being rebuffed by faculty and peers. These findings support previous literature on the experiences of Black women in the academy (Benjamin, 1997; Ellis, 2001;

Myers, 2002; Thomas & Hollenshead, 2001; Turner & Thompson, 1993). However, this study goes beyond most of the literature on Black female academics by emphasizing that the challenges encountered by the Black women emanate from hierarchical power relations based on race and gender. According to Black Feminist Thought and Political Race theories, race- and gender-based subjugation are employed to maintain unjust systems of power. Hence, the participants' experiences are mere interpersonal signifiers of how race and gender intolerance are embedded within the walls of academe. The very values and practices that would have prevented these Black women from entering their graduate programs 40 years ago remain, but have become less explicit. Thus, participants had to wrestle with raced and gendered micro-aggressions. These micro-aggressions were salient parts of their professional socialization experience.

Professional socialization is a cultural learning process that requires social interaction. It is about getting newcomers to learn the values and norms of a particular organization so that they understand how to meet organizational expectations. However, what happens when members of a subjugated group enter spaces that are defined by the norms and values of the dominant group? If traditional norms and values that undermine the legitimacy of Blacks and women are allowed to fester, then what remains is a professional socialization process that is reproductive rather than transformative. In other words, the structural constraints that existed prior to Civil Rights legislation are still present. Although manifested in subtle ways, these constraints still function to prevent raced groups from getting full access to resources within predominantly White institutions. As a result, they reproduce social norms that place women of color at the bottom of the power hierarchy.

It appears that the process of adapting and positioning may be difficult for Black women because the norms and values of academe are based upon the needs of White males (Caplan, 1993; Finkelstein, 1984). Rather than experiencing positive professional socialization, Black females are expected to accept their subordinate status through organizational acculturation—the process of adopting the norms and values of the dominant group.[3] In this study, the values of concern were those laden with notions of race and gender inferiority. The participants experienced dissonance because of misalignment between their self-worth and acts of superiority. It is dissonance that serves as the impetus for resistance, because the experience of disequilibrium is a reminder of one's social location. In their resistance, the participants challenged tenets of academe that are used to justify their exclusion. Most importantly, the women confronted narrow views of merit and epistemology by interpolating their lived experiences. In conjunction with the major findings (epistemological racism, lack of faculty and peer support, and tokenism) of this study, resistance to dominant narratives about merit and scholarship suggest ways that PWIs can deal with the politicization of race and gender in the teaching and learning environment, thereby attending to hostile climate issues.

As a whole, the raced and gendered experiences of the Black female graduate students in this study serve as warning signs of the dysfunctional aspects of academe. These warning signs provide an opportunity for predominantly White research institutions to look at ways that race, gender, and power intersect on campus. If the atmosphere is hostile or toxic for Black women, other people are exposed to that toxicity in varying degrees. Therefore, the racialized and gendered experiences of Black women help to identify institutional deficiencies that can be corrected through concerted efforts. Rather than viewing those experiences as simply an outgrowth of longstanding injustices, they should be viewed as catalysts for social change.

Notes

1. African American and Black are used interchangeably throughout this chapter.
2. Institutional racism occurs when institutions act as vehicles for discriminatory practices despite intentionality (Jones, 1972). It is typically covert and results from organizational structures, policies, and practices that favor one group and disadvantage another group (Chesler & Crowfoot, 2000). Social psychologist John Dovidio (2000) notes that after initial laws and practices are established, institutional racism survives through ritual, therefore intent to discriminate is not required.
3. Acculturation is the process of one cultural group adopting the culture of another group (Barker, 1999). However, it is generally used to refer to the relationship between nondominant and dominant cultural groups (Jensen, 1982; Kerka, 2003; Reynolds, 1992).

References

Alfred, M. V. (2001). Reconceptualizing marginality from the margins: Perspectives of African American tenured female faculty at a White research university. *Western Journal of Black Studies, 25*(1), 1–11.

Allen, B. J. (1995). *Twice blessed, doubly oppressed: Women of color in academe.* Paper presented at the Speech Communication Association, San Antonio, Texas.

Allen, W., Epps, E., Guillory, E., Suh, S., Bonous-Hammarth, M., & Stassen, M. (2002). Outsiders within. In W. Smith, P. Altbach & K. Lomotey (Eds.), *The racial crisis in American higher education.* Albany: State University of New York Press.

Anderson, J. (1988). *The education of Blacks in the south, 1860–1935.* Chapel Hill, North Carolina: The University of North Carolina Press.

Barker, R. L. (1999). *The social work dictionary.* Washington, DC: NASW Press.

Bell, D. (1995). Brown v board of education and the interest convergence dilemma. In K. Crenshaw, N. Gotanda, G. Peller, & K. Thomas (Eds.), *Critical race theory.* New York: The New Press.

Bell, D. (2004). *Silent covenants.* New York: Oxford University Press.

Bell, E. E., & Nkomo, S. (2001). *Our separate ways: Black and White women and the struggle for professional identity.* Boston: Harvard Business School Press.

Benjamin, L. (Ed.). (1997). *Black women in the academy.* Gainesville: University Press of Florida.

Cabrera, A., & Nasa, S. L. (Eds.). (2000). *Understanding the college choice of disadvantaged students.* San Francisco: Jossey-Bass Publishing.

Caplan, P. J. (1993). *Lifting a ton of feathers: A woman's guide to surviving in the academic world.* Toronto: University of Toronto Press.

Chesler, M., & Crowfoot, J. (2000). An organizational analysis of racism. In M. C. B. II (Ed.), *Organization and governance in higher education* (pp. 436–469). Boston, MA: Pearson Custom Publishing.

Clark, S. M., & Corcoran, M. (1986). Perspectives on the professional socialization of women faculty: A case of accumulative disadvantage? *The Journal of Higher Education, 57*(Jan-Feb), 20–43.

Constantine, M. G., & Watt, S. K. (2002). Cultural congruity, womanist identity attitudes, and life satisfaction among African American college women attending historically Black and predominantly White institutions. *Journal of College Student Development, 43*(2), 184–194.

Creswell, J. (1998). *Qualitative inquiry and research design.* Thousand Oaks: Sage.

Davis, A. (1981). *Women, race and class.* New York: Vintage Books.

Dovidio, J. (1997). 'Aversive' racism and the need for affirmative action. *The Chronicle of Higher Education, 43*(46), A60.

Dovidio, J. (2000). Racism. In A. E. Kazdin (Ed.), *Encyclopedia of psychology*. New York: Oxford University Press.

Dovidio, J. F., & Gaertner, S. L. (1998). Affirmative action, unintentional racial biases, and intergroup relations. *The Journal of Social Issues, 52*(4), 51.

Dunn, D., Rouse, L., & Seff, M. (1994). New faculty socialization in the academic workplace. In J. C. Smart (Ed.), *Higher education: Handbook of theory and research* (Vol. X, pp. 374–416). New York: Agathon Press.

Eberhardt, J. L., & Fiske, S. T. (Eds.). (1998). *Confronting racism*. Thousand Oaks, CA: Sage Publications.

Ellis, E. M. (2001). The impact of race and gender on graduate school socialization, satisfaction with doctoral study, and commitment to degree completion. *Western Journal of Black Studies, 25*(1), 30–45.

Evans, S. Y. (2007). *Black women in the ivory tower, 1850–1954*. Gainesville, FL: University Press of Florida.

Finkelstein, M. (1984). The status of academic women: An assessment of five competing explanations. *The Review of Higher Education, 7*(3), 223–246.

Giddings, P. (1984). *When and where I enter*. New York: William Morrow and Company, Inc.

Glazer-Raymo, J. (1999). *Shattering the myths: Women in academe*. Baltimore: The Johns Hopkins University Press.

Gregory, S. T. (1999). *Black women in the academy: The secrets to success and achievement*. Lanham: University Press of America.

Guba, E. G., & Lincoln, Y. S. (1982). Epistemological and methodological bases of naturalist inquiry. *Educational Communications and Technology Journal, 4*, 311–333.

Guinier, L., & Torres, G. (2002). *The miner's canary*. Cambridge: Harvard University Press.

Heyl, B. S. (2001). Ethnographic interviewing. In P. Atkinson, A. Coffey, S. Delamont, J. Lofland & L. Lofland (Eds.), *Handbook of ethnography*. London: Sage.

Higginbotham, E. B. (1992). African American women's history and the metalanguage of race. *Signs, 17*(2), 251–274.

Hill Collins, P. (2000). *Black feminist thought*. New York: Routledge.

Hine, D. C. (1995). Race and the inner lives of Black women in the west: Preliminary thoughts on the culture of dissemblance. In B. Guy-Sheftall (Ed.), *Words of fire*. New York: The New Press.

Hine, D. C., & Thompson, K. (1998). *A shining thread of hope*. New York: Broadway Books.

Holmes, S. L. (2001). *Narrated voices of African American women in academe*. Paper presented at the Association for the Study of Higher Education, Alabama.

Huang, G., Taddese, N., & Walter, E. (2000). *Entry and persistence of women and minorities in college science and engineering education, NCES 2000–601*. Washington, DC.

Jackson, L. (1998). The influence of both race and gender on the experiences of African American college women. *The Review of Higher Education, 21*(4), 359–375.

Jensen, K. (1982). Women's work and academic culture: Adaptations and confrontations. *Higher Education, 11*, 69–83.

Jones, J. (1972). *Prejudice and racism*. Reading, MA: Addison-Wesley Publishing.

Kanter, R. M. (1977). *Men and women of the corporation*. New York: Basic Books, Inc.

Kerka, S. (2003). *Career development of diverse populations. ERIC Digest.* (No. EDO-CE-03–249). Columbus, OH: ERIC Clearinghouse on Adult, Career, and Vocational Education.

King, D. (1995). Multiple jeopardy, multiple consciousness: The context of Black feminist ideology. In B. Guy-Sheftall (Ed.), *Words of fire* (pp. 294–318). New York: The New Press.

Krysan, M. (2000). Prejudice, politics, and public opinion: Understanding the sources of racial policy attitudes. *Annual Review of Sociology, 26*, 135–168.

McKay, N. (2002). A troubled peace: Black women in the halls of the White Academy. In L. Benjamin (Ed.), *Black women in the academy: Promises and perils* (pp. 11–22). Gainesville: University Press of Florida.

Myers, L. W. (2002). *A broken silence: Voices of African American women in the academy*. Westport, CT: Bergin & Garvey.

O'Connor, C. (2002). Black women beating the odds from one generation to the next: How the changing dynamics of constraint and opportunity affect the process of educational resilience. *American Educational Research Journal, 39*(4), 855–903.

Pascarella, E., & Terenzini, P. (1991). *How college effects students*. San Francisco: Jossey-Bass Publishers.

Reynolds, A. (1992). Charting the changes in junior faculty: Relationships among socialization, acculturation and gender. *The Journal of Higher Education, 63*(6), 637–652.

Rosser, S. V. (2004). *The science glass ceiling*. New York: Routledge.

Solorzano, D., & Ceja, M. (2000). Critical race theory, racial microaggressions, and campus racial climate: The experiences of African American college students. *Journal of Negro Education, 69*(Winter/Spring 2000), 60–73.

Strauss, A., & Corbin, J. (1998). *Basics of qualitative methods*. Thousand Oaks: Sage.

Sulé, V. T. (2008). *Black female faculty and professional socialization: Constraints, enablements and enactments*. Unpublished doctoral dissertation: University of Michigan, Ann Arbor.

Taylor, S. (2001). Locating and conducting discourse analytic research. In M. Wetherell, S. Taylor & S. Yates (Eds.), *Discourse as data: A guide for analysis* (pp. 5–48). Thousand Oaks: Sage.

Thomas, G. (2001). The dual role of scholar and social change agent: Reflections from tenured African American and Latina faculty. In R. Mabokela & A. L. Green (Eds.), *Sisters of the Academy*. Sterling, Virginia: Stylus Publishing.

Thomas, G., & Hollenshead, C. (2001). Resisting from the margins: The coping strategies of Black women and other women of color faculty members at a research university. *Journal of Negro Education, 70*(3), 166–175.

Tierney, W., & Bensimon, E. (1996). *Promotion and tenure: Community and socialization in academe*. Albany: State University of New York.

Tierney, W., & Rhoads, R. (1993). *Faculty socialization as a cultural process: A mirror of institutional commitment. ASHE-ERIC Higher Education Report No. 93–6*. Washington, DC: George Washington University.

Trower, C. (2002). *Women without tenure, part two: The gender sieve*. Retrieved October 2, 2005, from http://nextwave.sciencemag.org/cgi/content/full/2002/01/24/7

Trower, C., & Chait, R. (2002). Faculty diversity. *Harvard Magazine, March-April*, 23–28.

Turner, C. V., & Myers, S. (2000). *Faculty of color in academe*. Boston: Allyn and Bacon.

Turner, C. V., & Thompson, J. R. (1993). Socializing women doctoral students: Minority and majority experiences. *The Review of Higher Education, 16*(3), 355–370.

Van-Maanen, J., & Schein, E. H. (1979). Toward a theory of organizational socialization. In B. M. Staw (Ed.), *Research in organizational behavior*. Greenwich: JAI Press, Inc.

Villalpando, O., & Bernal, D. D. (2002). A critical race theory analysis of barriers that impede the success of faculty of color. In W. Smith, P. Altbach & K. Lomotey (Eds.), *The racial crisis in American higher education*. Albany: State University of New York Press.

Ward, K., & Bensimon, E. M. (2002). Socialization. In A. M. Martinez & K. A. Renn (Eds.), *Women in higher education: An encyclopedia* (pp. 431–435). Santa Barbara: ABC-CLIO.

Weiss, R. (1994). *Learning from strangers: The art and method of qualitative interview studies*. New York: Free Press.

Woods, R. L. (2001). Invisible women: The experiences of Black female doctoral students at the University of Michigan. In R. Mabokela & A. L. Green (Eds.), *Sisters of the academy* (pp. 105–116). Sterling, VA: Stylus.

7

DOES WHERE THEY START MATTER?

A Comparative Analysis of African American
Women Doctoral Recipients Who Started in a
Two-Year Versus a Four-Year Institution

Carolyn Buck

The fact that African American women historically have been and currently are underrepresented in graduate education and doctoral production is clear. According to the U.S. Department of Education National Center for Education Statistics (NCES) data, in 1976, African American women comprised 3.5% of all graduate students and 7.6% of all female graduate students, while earning 1.5% of all doctorates and 6% of doctorates awarded to women (U.S. Department of Education, NCES, 2007). By 2005, Black women totaled 7.6% of all graduate students and 12.7% of all female graduate students, while earning 7.4% of all doctoral degrees awarded to women and 3.6% of all doctorates awarded in 2005–2006. So, while they have made impressive gains in doctoral education, Black women are still underrepresented.

The degree of underrepresentation notwithstanding, little research has explored the paths African American women tread to reach the educational pinnacle of doctoral degree attainment and to enter into the American elite. This study examines this pathway in terms of the type of institution in which these women first enrolled. It compares African American women doctoral recipients who began at community colleges to those who began at four-year institutions. According to data from the Beginning Postsecondary Study,

African American women are more likely to begin their education at two-year colleges than are all students, including African American men (Walpole, 2008; Gafford Muhammad, 2007). Since they are more likely to begin at these institutions, and the increasing diversity within student bodies warrants increasing their representation in graduate education and doctoral degree attainment, this study explores these women's pathways through the community college to the doctorate. The chapter begins with an overview of trends in graduate enrollments and doctoral degree attainment, focusing specifically on trends among African American women. From there, the literature review includes a discussion of the role of community colleges in the education of diverse communities, issues of transfer, and pathways to the doctorate. The descriptive comparative analysis helps to address a vacuum in the literature regarding community colleges and terminal degree acquisition.

Trends in Doctoral Degree Attainment Among African American Women

From 1976 to 2005, the number of graduate students enrolled in U.S. universities increased from just over 1.3 million to nearly 2.2 million. Over that period, women increased their share of graduate enrollments from 46% to nearly 60% (NCES, 2007). As the enrollment of women in undergraduate education increased, the number of women in graduate school also increased and, since 1984, has grown to exceed the number of men (Berkner, Ho, & Cataldi 2002; NCES, 1999). African Americans also increased their share of graduate enrollments from 5.8% to 10.7%, and the enrollment of African American women increased from 3.5% to 7.6% over the same period (NCES, 2007). Given the comparatively larger share of African American women graduate students, compared to African Americans as a whole, as depicted in Figures 7.1 and 7.2, increases in African American women's share of graduate enrollment from 1976 to 2005 mirror increases in overall African American graduate enrollments. Data in Figures 7.1 through 7.4 are from NCES (2007).

The total number of doctorates has increased, with concomitant increases in graduate student enrollments. During the 1976–1977 school year, 33,126 doctorates were conferred. By 2005–2006, that number had grown to 56,076. As depicted in Figure 7.3, the share of doctorates earned

FIGURE 7.1
Percentage of Graduate Enrollments by Race

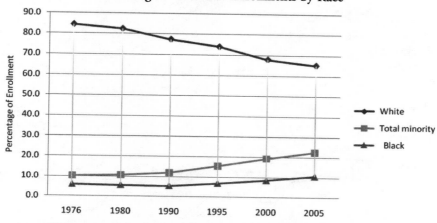

Distribution of Students by Race/Ethnicity, Selected Years 1976–2005

U.S. Department of Education, National Center for Education Statistics (NCES).

FIGURE 7.2
Percentage of Women's Graduate Enrollments by Race

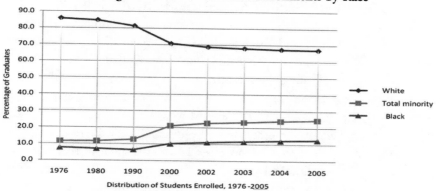

U.S. Department of Education, National Center for Education Statistics (NCES).

FIGURE 7.3
Doctoral Degrees Conferred by Race

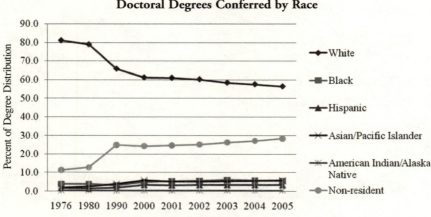

Distribution of Degrees 1976 Through 2005

U.S. Department of Education, National Center for Education Statistics (NCES).

by Whites has decreased over this period, while absolute numbers of doctor-ate have increased (more than doubled; see Figure 7.4). Blacks increased their number of doctorates by nearly threefold, Hispanics increased their numbers by a factor of nearly four, American Indians/Alaskan Natives doubled their numbers, and Asian/Pacific Islanders and nonresidents increased the number of doctorates earned by a factor of five. Doctoral completion rates of African Americans and Asian/Pacific Islanders have converged, while growth in the share of doctorates earned by Hispanics now surpasses that of Native Americans. Looking specifically at trends among women in Figure 7.4, they have increased their share from 24% of all doctoral earners to approximately 49%. Again, while the share of doctorates earned by White women has decreased, the overall numbers of doctorates have more than doubled. African American women slightly outpace Asian/Pacific Islander women in their share of doctorates, closely followed by Latinas. The number of Native American women earning doctorates remained flat, while the number of doctorates awarded to nonresident women more than doubled.

Among African American women, trends in doctoral completion rates are nonlinear, as depicted in Figure 7.5. There was a decrease in the number of doctorates earned during the mid-1990s and in African American women's share of doctorates, from 6% in 1976 to 4.3% in 1991. The rebound from the

FIGURE 7.4
Women's Doctoral Degrees Conferred by Race

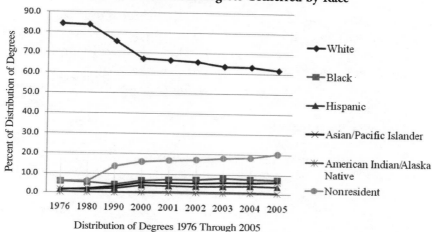

U.S. Department of Education, National Center for Education Statistics (NCES).

FIGURE 7.5
Share of Doctorates Conferred on African American Women

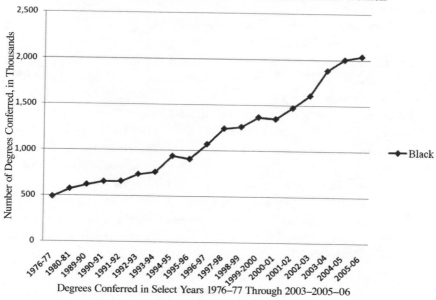

U.S. Department of Education, National Center for Education Statistics (NCES).

1990s was not linear, with increases between 1996–1997 and 1999–2000, which were followed by a decline in 2000–2001. While in 1997–1998 the share of doctorates earned exceeded 1976 levels, the 2005–2006 rate of 7.4% is a decline from an all-time high of 8.2% in 2003–2004. These declines in the share of doctorates conferred do not indicate an overall numerical loss, but are representative of periods of comparative stagnation, while the number and proportion of other non-White, non-U.S. women earning doctorates have increased.

This unevenness in doctoral degree completion is of concern and is perhaps linked to other experiences and challenges along the higher education pipeline. In particular, this analysis focuses on African American women students' entry into higher education and whether there is a relationship between starting postsecondary studies at a (two-year) community college or a four-year institution and subsequently completing those studies with a doctoral degree.

Review of the Literature

Community colleges enrolled 35% of all college students in 2006–2007 (Provasnik & Planty, 2008). While community college students are diverse in terms of race, ethnicity, and socioeconomic status, they are also of disproportionately nontraditional ages, from low-income backgrounds, African American or Latino, and are more likely than college students as a whole to require remedial education (Boswell & Wilson, 2004; Provasnik & Planty, 2008). In this vein, community colleges are perhaps the most pluralistic of all higher education institutions in the United States. This may be because this was their intended design—to serve the needs and interests of U.S. communities. However, those needs have changed over time, from being the early transitional secondary to postsecondary "junior" colleges of the 1900s to colleges of first resort for many students, regardless of economic status, including those not completing high school (Cohen & Brawer, 2003).

In 2008, 46%—nearly half—of all African American undergraduates began their education at community colleges (American Association of Community Colleges [AACC], 2008). African American women are more likely than are their male counterparts to begin their education at community colleges (NCES, 2007), yet little research has been done on African Americans in community colleges, and almost none has been specific to African American women (Lewis & Middleton, 2003). The community college's vocational mission is well documented, and much of the research that has focused specifically on African American women in community colleges explores these women's ability to secure employment as a result of attendance (McAtee & Benshoff, 2006; Valadez, 1993).

Although not all students who enter community colleges intend to complete a degree or transfer, graduation rates are generally lower than at four-year institutions and attrition rates are higher (Provasnik & Planty, 2008). Further, a minority of students who begin at community colleges with the intent of transferring actually do so (Boswell & Wilson, 2004; Coley, 2000; Hagedorn, Moon, Cypers, Maxwell, & Lester, 2006; Rifkin, 1996; Townsend & Wilson, 2006). Scholars have found that the students who are most likely to transfer are traditional age, have high socioeconomic status (SES), and are disproportionately White and Asian American students who required the fewest remedial classes (Dougherty & Kienzl, 2006; Townsend & Wilson, 2006), while African American students are among the least likely to transfer (Hagedorn et al., 2006; Melguizo, 2007).

There are many reasons for the low transfer rates, including a lack of effective collaborative relationships and the need for increased faculty involvement (Kisker, 2007). Community college supporters also point to students' diverse enrollment intentions, high remedial needs, and unique characteristics when explaining their low graduation and transfer rates (Coley, 2000; Hagedorn et al., 2006; Townsend & Wilson, 2006). However, critics of the two-year college system maintain that attendance at a two-year community college may not improve a student's chance to cross class and social boundaries in a highly stratified social system (Brint & Karabel, 1989; Dougherty, 1994). In fact, Pascarella and Terenzini (2005) posit that starting at a community college actually lowers a student's chances of attaining a bachelor's degree. Critics' arguments notwithstanding, the two-year college may be the only place in the postsecondary arena that can provide the needed skills and development of social, human, and cultural competencies that will ensure success when students transition to four-year campuses.

The transition from the two-year campus to the baccalaureate-granting institution may be difficult for many students because they do not know how to negotiate the higher education system (Hagedorn et al., 2006). When compared with students who started at four-year institutions, two-year institution enrollees are less prepared (Boswell & Wilson, 2004; Coley, 2000;

Rifkin, 1996). As high school students, these individuals acquired less knowledge about planning for college and how to move through the maze of higher education once they did matriculate.

In addition to their limited academic achievement, students attending community college are often disadvantaged in access to the human, social, and cultural capital that could support them in navigating the educational system (Bourdieu & Jean, 1977; Coleman, 1988; Rhoades & Valadez, 1996; Smith, 1993; Valadez, 1993). According to this line of research, students from socioeconomically privileged backgrounds have access to their parents' acquired education and the associated benefits of income, possessions, and ongoing social interaction. Therefore, they acquire a higher level of skills, knowledge, and ability by virtue of the familiar setting and the types of daily interactions they experience. Perhaps students who successfully transfer from community colleges already possess this capital, or perhaps they acquire it while attending these institutions. Regardless of the reason, given the low transfer rates from community colleges to four-year institutions, students who do manage to transfer are resilient. Furthermore, students who start at two-year colleges and eventually earn their doctorate degrees must be particularly resilient, and educators can learn much from exploring their paths and characteristics.

While research on institutional origins of doctorate recipients has found that students who attend more-selective institutions as undergraduates are more likely to obtain a doctoral degree (Buck, 2003; Solorzano, 1995; Tidball, 1986; Tidball, Smith, Tidball, & Wolf-Wendel, 1999; Wolf, 1995), little research specifically connects attendance at a two-year community college with doctoral degree attainment. This dearth is despite the fact that such research on the doctoral pipeline has taken place on other specific types of originating institutions, such as women's colleges, historically Black colleges and universities (HBCUs), co-educational institutions, and Ivy League schools (Guy-Sheftall & Bell Scott, 1989; Hulbert & Schuster, 1993; Lind, 1995; Solorzano, 1995; Wolf, 1995). Additionally, little research has examined the institutional origins of successful African American women who earn doctorates, even though Wolf-Wendel (1998) found institutional criteria to be the most significant factor in predicting the success of women who pursue graduate education.

For White women, baccalaureate origins at small, single-sex, selective, private institutions were associated more highly with success in graduate programs. For Latinas, however, selectivity was negatively associated with graduate educational success, whereas for African American women, institutional selectivity was a neutral factor (Wolf-Wendel, 1998). Since African American women are more likely to enter the educational pipeline at the community college level, research on doctoral recipients who started at community colleges addresses multiple gaps in the literature and is critical to understanding the educational trajectories of these resilient women.

Methodology

This study is part of a larger exploratory study highlighting factors that differentiate among the dependent variables of point of entry, type of employment, and income and the predictor variables of gender, race, father's and mother's education level, level of debt, and types of educational institutions attended (Buck, 2003). The larger study was a quantitative analysis of secondary data pertaining to recipients whose initial point of entry into postsecondary education was a two-year or associate degree–granting institution, compared to four-year origin recipients. The reference group was two-year college attendees. The present analysis focuses on the trajectories of African American women. In this study, the term *two-year* is used interchangeably with the term *community college*. For the purpose of the study, any institution accredited to award the associate in arts or associate in science as its highest degree is a community college (Cohen & Brawer, 2003). This includes comprehensive two-year colleges and many technical institutions as well.

Data Sets

The time frame for the study was 1988–1995, and the Survey of Earned Doctorates (SED) was used as the secondary database. The National Opinion Research Council (NORC) maintains the SED as part of the Doctoral Records File for the National Science Foundation (NSF). The initial respondents for this study completed the SED at the point of completing their doctoral study between 1989 and 1995. The population for the SED is all individuals receiving a research doctorate from a U.S. academic institution in the 12-month period ending June 30. Racial and ethnic groups included in the larger study were Asian, Black, Hispanic/Latino, Caucasian, and American Indian. Initial selection for the study was based on whether the recipients were U.S. citizens and initially completed the SED. Men and women with a code for JRCOLL, indicating whether they attended a two-year college or received an associate degree from a two-year institution, were included. The recipients' choices were described using their responses to the survey questions about their level of debt and demographic data when completing the SED.

The data population represents a census of all graduates who earned degrees from regionally accredited U.S. universities in all fields. The SED data files represent census data for all doctoral recipients, and the subgroups are represented in the same proportions in which they would be found in the normal population. The current study focuses on African American women within the larger data set.

Method of Analysis

The focus of this research was two questions related to differences in background characteristics and the pathway to the terminal degree. The questions sought to describe the recipients and how they moved along the educational pathway from the initial point of entry to acquiring the terminal degree. The questions were,

- What are the background characteristics that distinguish African American female doctoral recipients who began at a two-year and four-year college/university, taking into consideration selected demographic variables?
- What are African American female doctoral recipients' primary and secondary sources of support and level of debt incurred from point of entry to degree completion?

Descriptive statistics are used to examine these questions for the current study.

Data Sample

For the purpose of this research study, a data sample was extracted that included only those respondents under 60 years of age whose terminal degree completion was between 1988 and 1995. The total sample was 147,058 cases. A cross-tabulation of point of entry, race, and gender is presented in Table 7.1. Cross-tabulations for the universe of African American women by point of entry are presented in Table 7.2. The race and gender distribution for the entire data sample was as follows: 626 American Indians (.4%); 5,037 Blacks (3.6%); 4,164 Asian-Pacific Islanders (3.0%); 3,938 Hispanic (2.8%); 125,545

TABLE 7.1

Race by Gender by Point of Origin Cross Tabulation

Race	Point of College Origin								
	2-year			4-year			Total		
	Male	Female	Total	Male	Female	Total	Male	Female	Total
Count									
American Indian	65	60	125	271	230	501	336	290	626
Asian/Pacific Islander	189	94	283	2,515	1,366	3,881	2,704	1,460	4,164
Black/African American	240	333	573	1,790	2,674	4,464	2,030	3,007	5,037
Hispanic	349	298	647	1,728	1,563	3,291	2,077	1,861	3,938
White	8,070	5,787	13,857	64,031	47,657	111,688	72,101	53,444	125,545
Other/Multi	30	16	46	244	138	382	274	154	428
Percent within entry									
American Indian	52.0%	48.0%	100.0%	54.10%	45.9%	100.0%	53.7%	46.3%	100.0%
Asian/Pacific Islander	66.8%	33.3%	100.0%	64.80%	35.2%	100.0%	64.9%	35.1%	100.0%
Black/African American	41.9%	58.1%	100.0%	40.10%	59.9%	100.0%	40.3%	59.7%	100.0%
Hispanic	53.9%	46.1%	100.0%	52.50%	47.5%	100.0%	52.7%	47.3%	100.0%
White	58.2%	41.8%	100.0%	57.30%	42.7%	100.0%	57.4%	42.6%	100.0%
Other/Multi	65.2%	34.8%	100.0%	63.90%	36.1%	100.0%	64.0%	36.0%	100.0%
Percent within gender									
American Indian	19.3%	20.7%	20.0%	80.70%	79.35%	80.00%	100.0%	100.0%	100.0%
Asian/Pacific Islander	7.0%	6.4%	6.8%	93.0%	93.6%	93.2%	100.0%	100.0%	100.0%
Black/African American	11.8%	11.1%	11.4%	88.2%	88.9%	88.6%	100.0%	100.0%	100.0%
Hispanic	16.8%	16.0%	16.4%	83.25%	84.05%	83.6%	100.0%	100.0%	100.0%
White	11.2%	10.8%	11.0%	88.80%	89.2%	89.0%	100.0%	100.0%	100.0%
Other/Multi	10.9%	10.4%	10.7%	89.10%	89.6%	89.3%	100.0%	100.0%	100.0%
Percent within total									
American Indian	10.4%	9.6%	20.0%	43.30%	36.7%	80.00%	53.7%	46.7%	100.0%
Asian/Pacific Islander	4.5%	2.3%	6.8%	60.40%	32.8%	93.2%	64.9%	35.1%	100.0%
Black/African American	4.8%	6.8%	11.4%	35.5%	53.1%	88.6%	40.3%	59.7%	100.0%
Hispanic	8.9%	7.6%	16.45%	43.95%	39.7%	83.6%	52.7%	47.3%	100.0%
White	6.4%	4.5%	11.0%	51.00%	38.0%	89.0%	57.4%	42.6%	100.0%
Other/Multi	7.0%	3.7%	10.7%	57.0%	32.2%	89.3%	64.0%	36.0%	100.0%

Missing = 7320 (5%)

TABLE 7.2
Point of Entry for African American Women

		Point of Entry					
		4-year		2-year		Total	
		Women	Total	Women	Total	Women	Total
All women	Count	51179	51179	6278	6278	57457	57457
	Percent within 2 & 4 year	89.1%	89.1%	10.9%	10.9%	100.0%	100.0%
	Percent within women	100.0%	100.0%	100.0%	100.0%	100.0%	100.0%
African American women	Count	2674	2674	333	333	3007	3007
	Percent within 2 & 4 year	88.9%	88.9%	11.1%	11.1%	100.0%	100.0%
	Percent within All African American women identified	100.0%	100.0%	100.0%	100.0%	100.0%	100.0%

Missing = 2826 (4.5%)

Caucasians (88.9%); and 428 other/multiple race (.3%), and approximately 5% were missing (Table 7.1).

Variables

The variables used in the analyses are presented in the Appendix, along with the levels of measurement and variable transformations. The Doctoral Records Files are composed of character/categorical data, and SED data files are primarily categorical data files with nominal and ordinal data. As a result, several data transformations were required to facilitate the descriptive analysis. Variables were recoded to numeric scale and/or dummy coded or both. Variables examined as descriptors include age, region of college entry, race/ethnicity, gender, primary source of support, secondary source of support, parents' combined level of education, father's education level, mother's education level, type of doctoral institution (B.A. Carnegie, M.A. Carnegie, Ph.D. Carnegie, HBCU), time to degree, and level of debt. Several of the variables required further recoding and are explained below.

Age. The working database file for the SED included questions related to age, but the age variable was missing in the SED database release. Using the data transformation process, the variable age was created by subtracting the birth month and year from the survey year and month—April 15, 1995. The variable age group 1993 (agegrp93) was recoded using intervals of five.

Region of college entry. The variable was transformed using the state codes for the 50 states into the 9 NORC-designated regions; they are New England, Middle Atlantic, East North Central, West North Central, South Atlantic, East South Central, West South Central, Mountain, and Pacific.

Race/ethnicity. The 9 levels of race/ethnicity were collapsed into five because some of the race identifiers generated small expected cell values. The racial codes for Puerto Rican, Mexican American, and other Hispanic were combined and resulted in 4,161 Hispanics (2.9%) of the working database. In terms of gender, 79,522 recipients identified themselves as men (53.7%), 60,216 were identified as women (46.3%), and 3,007 (2% of the total) were African American women. Of this last group, 333 (11.1%) started their postsecondary education at a two-year institution or community college.

Sources of support (primary source of support and secondary source of support). The variables "primary and secondary source of support" were indicated by a two-digit code for 1990 to the present and a code and percentage for 1987–1989. Thirty-one item responses for source of support from the survey were used in the data input. In this study, the variables for primary (first source of financial support) and secondary (second source of financial support), as identified by survey respondents, were used in all analysis related to support. NORC suggested clustering the responses into four categories for ease of analysis. As a result, the four areas of support for primary and secondary sources of support are personal support, university support, federal support, and awards.

Parents' combined level of education. The variable combined level of parents' education was computed using the combined variables of father's and mother's education levels. Instead of multiple levels for grammar school, grammar levels 1–11 were collapsed into code "A," indicating "less than high school." The remaining variable codes were recoded into four levels of education for the variables father's and mother's education level, followed by the calculation of the combined level of education for parents.

Types of institution (B.A., M.A., Ph.D.). The 19 codes for the variables BACARN, MACARN, and PhDCARN were recoded into Type of Carnegie Institution and then collapsed and recoded into either Research I or Doctoral I. The Carnegie classification system used in these descriptive analyses is the original Carnegie classification framework, now called basic classification. As of 2005, a new system of classification was established. The use of Research I and II last appeared in the 1994 doctoral records data.

Level of debt. This variable represents the recipients' indication of the level of debt incurred during their undergraduate and/or graduate school enrollment. The 12 codes for the variable DEBTLEVL used between 1988 and 1996 were recoded in the transformed variable DEBTLRV resulting in the levels of debt being no response; some debt; less than $10,000; less than $30,000; less than $40,000; and $40,000 or more.

Results and Discussion

Demographics

The African American women included in this study had a mean age of 42.82 or 43 years. For two-year-entry African American women, the mean age was 44.78 or 45 years, while for four-year-entry African American doctoral recipients, the mean age was 42.56 or 43 years. Two-year-entry African American women doctorate recipients were slightly older than their four-year counter-parts. The mean time to degree completion from the point of entry into postsecondary education until the completion of the degree was 13.10 years, with 6 years being the minimum and 30 the maximum number of years—*SD* = 3.89 for two-year-entry African American women doctorates. In comparison, the mean time to degree for four-year-entry African American women was 12.84 or 13 years—*SD* = 3.63. For the total population of African American women doctorates, the mean time to degree was 12.87 or 13 years—*SD* = 3.66. The two-year-entry women doctorate recipients took slightly longer to move through the system from their first undergraduate institution to earning their doctorate. This study does not include data for how many times a recipient may have stopped out between degrees or during completion of a degree; rather, this number represents actual time in college.

The regions of entry for the majority of the African American two-year-entry recipients were East North Central, 86 (25.8%); Pacific, 60 (18%); South Atlantic, 54 (16.2%); East Central, 41 (12.3%); and Middle Atlantic, 40 (12%). The remaining recipients were dispersed among other regions. For the African American women who first entered college at a four-year institution, the regions of entry for the majority were South Atlantic, 875 (32.7%); East North Central, 399 (14.9%); East South Central, 350 (13.1%); and East North Central, 399 (14.9%), with the remaining recipients representing other regions.

While the women may have matriculated in different regions of the country, they all relied heavily on personal resources to finance their education. I describe the recipients' primary and secondary sources of education in the next section of the analysis.

Primary Source of Support

When asked about the primary source of support during their graduate study, 46.5% of all doctoral recipients who began at two-year colleges, and 37.9% of all doctoral recipients who began at four-year institutions, responded that their primary sources of support were loans, family members, and earnings/contributions. Among African American women two-year-entry doctoral award recipients, that figure swelled to 52.9%. Only 11.7% of African American doctorate recipients accessed university support through university fellowships, traineeships, and/or department of education-administered fellowships. Of all the doctoral award recipients who began at two-year institutions, 3.6% funded their education with federal assistance, and 5.6% of recipients who began four-year colleges reported using federal assistance. In comparison, 5.1% of all African American women reported using federal assistance. Less than 1% of two-year-entry African American women doctoral recipients and 1.4% of their four-year counterparts indicated that their primary source of support was from awards.

Secondary Source of Support

The recipients' secondary source of support was similar to their primary source of support. Among all African American women, 165 (49.5%) indicated that their secondary source of support was personal. Thirty-five percent of two-year-entry African American doctoral award recipients indicated that their secondary source of support was in the form of university fellowships, traineeships, and/or department of education-administered fellowships. This figure is substantially higher than that for the general two-year entry population, wherein 21% indicated that their secondary source of support was in the form of fellowships, traineeships, and/or department of education-administered fellowships.

Debt Level

Fifty-three percent of all two-year-entry doctorate recipients incurred some level of debt, in comparison to 88% of four-year-entry doctorate recipients. The majority of the recipients had less than $20,000 in debt. The amount of debt two-year-entry African American women incurred while completing the degree ranged from zero to more than $30,000 (see Table 7.3). Among doctoral award recipients with zero to $10,000 of debt, 10.6% (11,054) began their college education at a two-year institution, and 89% (92,916) were four-year-entry doctoral award recipients. In comparison, approximately 67% of African American women doctorate recipients who started in a two-year institution had less than $10,000 of debt. Approximately 83% of two-year-entry African American women doctoral recipients had less than $20,000 in debt, and a small group of these recipients (5%) did not indicate their level of debt, stating only that they had incurred debt. By comparison, 38% of four-year-entry African American women had incurred no debt, and 31% had incurred less than $10,000 of debt. As a point of contrast, 24 (.0%) of all two-year entry doctorate recipients and 0.1% of all four-year-entry doctorate recipients indicated that they had incurred debt during undergraduate and/or graduate study, but did not give a specific amount. However, 89 (3.3%)

TABLE 7.3
African American Women's Debt by Point of Origin

Point of Origin	Missing	No Debt	Less than $10,000	Less than $20,000	Less than $30,000	$40,000 or More	Yes Debt	Total
	42	1008	838	424	272	89	1	2674
Percent of 4 year	1.6%	37.7%	31.3%	15.9%	10.2%	3.3%	0%	100.0%
2 year	4	133	89	54	31	21	1	333
Percent of 2 year	1.4%	39.9%	26.7%	16.2%	9.3%	6.3%	.3%	100.0%

Missing = 207

of the four-year-entry African American women doctorate holders incurred more than $40,000 of debt versus 21 (6.3%) of the two-year-entry African American women.

Debt loads among two-year-entry African American women doctorate recipients may be directly connected to their use of personal finances. Research has shown that African American and ethnically diverse women use the community college as their first point of entry because it is economically more feasible than a four-year institution (Brint & Karabel, 1989; Cohen & Brawer, 2003; Dougherty, 1994). Many African American women may have been first-generation college students and lacked the fiscal resources to finance their education (Johnson, 2001). Moreover, the recipients are older and are more likely to have been working as they pursued their studies (Buck, 2003; Johnson, 2001). Although these data do not reveal access to financial assistance, they appear to signal a comparatively larger amount of personal work needed to finance degree completion.

Doctorate Completion by Institution

At the point of completing doctorates, 191 (57.9%) of two-year-entry African American women doctorates attained the degree at Research I/II institutions, followed by 129 (39.1%) completing the degree at Doctoral I/II institutions, 9 (2.7%) at Master's I/II institution, and a small percentage (.3%) of the group completing their studies at Medical institutions. In contrast, 1,843 (69.2%) four-year-entry African American women doctorates completed the degree at a Research institution, followed by 763 (28.7%) who completed the degree at a Doctoral institution. A smaller percentage of these four-year-entry women completed doctorates at Master's (2.7%) and Medical institutions (.3%) (see Table 7.4).

It is interesting to note the patterns of access for African American women as they moved from undergraduate degree completion to doctoral completion. African American women doctorates from two-year institutions were more likely to have completed their baccalaureate degree at either a Master I/II (44.2%) or Research I/II (31.9%) institution versus African American women from four-year institutions, who completed their B.A./B.S. at either a Master's I/II (35.5%) or Research I/II (29.3%). At the point of completing the master's degree, two-year-entry women were less likely to have completed the degree at a Research I/II. Specifically, 45% of two-year-entry women graduated from a Research I/II institution, compared to the

TABLE 7.4
Doctoral Institution by Point of Entry

	Doctoral Type of Institution									
	Research I/II		Doctoral I/II		Master's I/II		Medical		Total	
	4-year	2-year	4-year	2-year	4-year	2-year	4-year	2-year	4-year	2-year
					Point of Entry					
African American										
Men and women	3181	359	1125	184	94	11	46	8	4446	562
Percent within race	71.5%	63.9%	25.3%	32.7%	2.1%	2.0%	1.0%	1.4%	100.0%	100.0%
Women only	1843	191	763	129	54	9	2	1	2662	330
Percent within point of entry	69.2%	57.9%	28.7%	39.1%	2.0%	2.7%	.1%	.3%	100.0%	100.0%

majority (51.3%) of African American women from four-year institutions. Two-year-entry women were more likely to complete the master's degree at either a Doctoral I/II (23.3%) or Masters I/II (29.7%) institution. In contrast, four-year-entry African American women were less likely to complete the master's degree at a Doctoral institution (21%) or a Master's institution (25%) than were two-year-entry women. Both two- and four-year-entry African American women were more likely to complete the master's degree at a Research I/II, followed by completion at a Master's I/II, then a Doctoral I/II or Medical institution (see Table 7.5).

Historically Black Colleges and Universities

Smaller percentages of African American women completed their undergraduate, master's, and doctorate degrees at a historically Black college or university. Prior to the completion of the doctorate, 14.1% of two-year-entry women completed undergraduate degrees at an HBCU versus 43% of four-year-entry women. Thirty-one (9.3%) two-year-entry women completed their master's degree at a HBCU, in contrast to 459 (17.2%) of African American women from four-year colleges. Twenty-four (7.2%) two-year-entry African American women doctorates completed those degrees at HBCUs, compared to 239 (8.9%) African American women from four-year colleges (see Table 7.6).

Of note, in the larger study, approximately 6% of all African Americans whose initial point of entry was a two-year college completed their doctoral study at a HBCU. A comparable proportion, approximately 8%, of all four-year-entry African-American men and women doctoral awardees completed doctorates at HBCUs (Buck, 2003). However, for this study, there appears to be a slightly higher percentage of African American women from four-year colleges who completed their doctoral degrees at HBCUs, compared to all African Americans who began at four-year institutions. Similarly, a slightly higher percentage of African American women from two-year institutions (7.2%) completed doctorates at HBCUs, compared to all African Americans who began at two-year colleges.

Combined Parents' Level of Education

For African-American women doctorate recipients whose point of entry was a two-year college, the combined parent education level reflects that of the larger data sample. Ninety-four (28.2%) of the parents had less than a junior

TABLE 7.5
Patterns of Carnegie Institution Attendance for Two-and Four-year Women

Carnegie Classification	Baccalaureate Carnegie			Master's Carnegie			Doctoral Carnegie		
	Two-year	Four-year	Total	Two-year	Four-year	Total	Two-year	Four-year	Total
Research I/II	104	770	874	141	1269	1410	191	1843	2034
% of Research I/II	31.9%	29.3%	29.6%	45.0%	51.3%	50.6%	57.9%	69.2%	68.0%
Doctoral I/II	48	277	325	73	542	615	129	763	892
% of Doctoral I/II	14.7%	10.5%	11.1%	69.1%	21.9%	22.1%	39.1%	28.7%	29.8%
Masters I/II	144	931	1075	93	621	714	9	54	63
% of Masters I/II	44.2%	35.5%	36.4%	29.7%	25.1%	25.6%	2.7%	2.0%	2.1%
Medical	30	648	678	6	42	48	1	2	3
% of Medical	9.2%	24.7%	23.0%	1.9%	1.7%	1.7%	.3%	.1%	.1%
Total	326	2626	2952	313	2474	2787	330	2662	2992
% of Total	100.0%	100.0%	100.0%	100.0%	100.0%	100.0%	100.0%	100.0%	100.0%
Missing	262		8.2%	427		13.3%	222		6.9%

TABLE 7.6
Point of Entry by Historically Black Colleges and Universities (HBCUs)

	Baccalaureate HBCU			Master's HBCU			Doctorate HBCU		
	HBCU	Non HBCU	Total	HBCU	Non-HBCU	Total	HBCU	Non-HBCU	Total
4-year women	1150	1524	2674	459	2215	2674	239	2435	2674
% of 4 year	43%	57.0%	100.0%	17.2%	82.8%	100.0%	8.9%	91.1%	100.0%
2-year women	47	286	333	31	302	333	24	309	333
% of 2 year	14.1%	85.9%	100.0%	9.3%	90.7%	100.0%	7.2%	92.8%	100.0%
Total	1197	1810	3007	490	2517	3007	263	2744	3007
% of Total	39.8%	60.2%	100.0%	16.3%	83.7%	100.0%	8.7%	91.3%	100.0%

high school education, and 68 (20.4%) had completed high school only. Parents of all African American doctorates, men and women, from both two-year and four-year institutions had limited experience with college- and graduate-level work. Forty-four (13.2%) completed college and 8 (2.4%) completed a master's level degree. None of the parents of African American women doctorates, either two-year- or four-year-entry, had achieved a doctoral degree (see Table 7.7).

This chapter described African American women who began their higher education at a two-year college compared to a four-year college and subsequently earned a doctorate. Overall, 11% of all doctoral degree recipients began their postsecondary education in community colleges. This is true of men and women generally, and it is also true of African American women. An analysis of doctoral institution types and patterns of degree completion strongly indicated that the largest group of women, whether they began at two- or four-year colleges, earned doctorates at research institutions, followed by doctoral institutions. African American women used several different options, such as Master's or Doctoral institutions between the point of origin and acquisition of the doctoral degree. The largest group of women from both two- and four-year institutions completed the B.A./B.S. degree at Master's I/II institutions, and completed the master's degree at Research I/II institutions.

TABLE 7.7
Parents' Combined Education Level

Valid	Frequency	Percent	Valid Percent	Cumulative Percent
Zero to junior high	94	28.2	29.4	29.4
Less than high school	49	14.7	15.3	44.7
High school	68	20.4	21.3	65.9
Less than college	41	12.3	12.8	78.8
College	44	13.2	13.8	92.5
Less than graduate degree	14	4.2	4.4	96.9
Master's Professional	8	2.4	2.5	99.4
Less than Ph.D.	2	.6	.6	
Total	320	96.1		
Missing	13	3.9		
Total	333	100.0	100.0	100.0

Missing = 13

Two-year-entry respondents had less debt, were older, and were more likely to fund doctoral studies through personal resources rather than with federal, state, or loan resources, as did those from four-year institutions. The primary sources of support for 46.5% of two-year-entry doctoral recipients and for 37.9% of four-year-entry doctoral recipients was loans, family members, and earnings/contributions. However, African American women who began at a two-year college were more likely to use personal financial resources and incur lower levels of debt. Of particular significance was the finding that African American women in this study did not have parents who knew what it takes to earn a doctoral degree. Thus, the majority of the women doctorates lacked access to the social and cultural capital that comes with having parents who have a working knowledge of higher education and a tangible appreciation of the associated benefits of education. Yet, they were able to remain tenacious and resilient in their pursuit of the degree.

Research in professional education and doctoral production indicates that Research I and Liberal Arts institutions are the primary paths to a terminal degree for those who earn a doctoral degree (Solorzano, 1995; Tidball, 1986; Tidball et al., 1999; Wolf, 1995). This trend proved to be consistent for recipients whose initial point of entry was a four-year institution. In terms of academic planning for all two-year institution attendees, there may be a need for counselors and administrators in both community colleges and four-year institutions to assess students' career and academic goals in terms of the potential institutional path for future graduate-level work. African American women who start in a two-year institution are less likely to move along the pathway to the terminal degree in proportionately representative numbers in comparison to White men and women with two-year starts. Like their White counterparts, doctoral award recipients from ethnically diverse backgrounds are more likely to have attended a four-year institution. Yet, the largest numbers of African-Americans are entering higher education by way of two-year institutions. These students will need closer monitoring through support programs and advising to move from the two-year programs into programs at the four-year level that will support their studies and ensure that they move along the pathway to terminal degree completion.

Conclusion

To ensure the success of all two-year college attendees, particularly African American women, policy makers and administrators should institutionalize programs that connect students from their initial institutions to potential transfer institutions. In addition, institutions within state systems of higher education should be encouraged to collaborate in establishing mentoring and academic support programs that closely link two-year college women with four-year colleges. Some suggested actions are as follows:

- Develop articulation/transfer degrees that build a network of support between public school and two- and four-year institutions.
- Recognize that community colleges are a financially smart way to finance a student's education. As noted in this study, African American women starting in two-year institutions who earned doctorates had less debt on completing their degree than did their four-year counterparts.
- Strengthen students' basic skills before they arrive on a college campus and alert them before graduation about the skills and resilience necessary for college success. Research has documented that community college women of African American descent may require intrusive intervention and support to be successful as they prepare to enter a four-year institution (Boswell & Wilson, 2004; Provasnik & Planty, 2008). This intervention may be done by developing and supporting peer advisor programs and academic advancement courses for high school students who have the desire to transfer.
- Assist African American women students in developing relationships on and off campus that support their educational and career goals and enable them to strengthen their social and cultural capital. Community women, faculty, and staff can serve as mentors and career guides to support these women as they move through the academic pipeline. This process is most important because it will facilitate African American women's ability to remain resilient and tenacious as they pursue their studies.
- Pursue efforts to acquaint students at the two-year level with graduate school possibilities, especially opportunities for research projects, if they are interested in pursuing a terminal degree. Community college women, and African American women specifically, need to have advocates to assist them in developing research skills.

The critical point this research raises relates to the fact that nearly half of African Americans who enter postsecondary education matriculate at the nation's two-year colleges (AACC, 2008). The reasons for their entry vary, but they often cite the high cost of college (sticker and actual prices). Yet another factor might be higher admission standards in four-year colleges as well as the overall decline of remediation efforts at these institutions. Given these possible factors, the recruitment of future African American women doctoral candidates should begin at the two-year college. Beyond recruitment, efforts should be made to encourage students to persist to doctoral degree completion. The growing number of women and ethnically diverse populations who are matriculating at two-year institutions will require different types of support programs to ensure their successful transition through the pipeline. Critical to the success of future African American women graduates and doctorate earners will be access to accurate information, vision of the future, and opportunities to learn what it takes to start college and transition through to the terminal degree.

More data on the doctoral path of African American women who start their higher education at a community college are needed than what the secondary data used in this investigation provided. These secondary data did not provide critical information related to transfer and general education status at the point of leaving the two-year institution. Studies that replicate the baccalaureate origins studies (e.g., Wolf-Wendel, 1998) using two-year institutions as the point of reference are recommended. While community colleges may be the point of entry for most African American women (U.S. Department of Education, NCES, 2007), their numbers are not reflected in the pool of transfers at the baccalaureate level or in graduate programs for master's and terminal degrees. This deficit is a challenge for the system, and a concerted effort must be made to support the efforts of two-year institutions as points of entry for African American women who may be eligible for the doctoral pipeline.

References

American Association of Community Colleges (AACC). (2008). AACC research and statistics. Retrieved August 14, 2008, from http://www2.aacc.nche.edu/research/index.htm

Berkner, L., Ho, S., & Cataldi, E. F. (2002). *Descriptive summary of 1995–96 beginning postsecondary students: Six years later. Statistical analysis report.* (NCES 2003–151). Washington, DC: NCES, U.S. Department of Education.

Boswell, K., & Wilson, C. D. (2004). *Keeping America's promise: A report on the future of the community college.* Denver, CO: Education Commission of the States.

Bourdieu, P., & Jean, C. P. (1977). *Reproduction in education, society and culture.* Beverly Hills, CA: Sage Publications.

Brint, S., & J. Karabel. (1989). *The diverted dream: Community colleges and the promise of educational opportunity in America, 1900–1985.* New York: Oxford University Press.

Buck, C. E. B. (2003). *Does where they start matter? A comparative analysis of doctoral recipients who started in a two- versus a four-year institution.* Unpublished doctoral dissertation, The Claremont Graduate University, Claremont, CA.

Cohen, A. M., & Brawer, F. B. (2003). *The American community college* (4th ed.). San Francisco, CA: Jossey-Bass.

Coleman, J. S. (1988). Social capital in the creation of human capital. *American Journal of Sociology, 94,* 95–120.

Coley, R. J. (2000). *The American community college turns 100: A look at its students, programs, and prospects.* Princeton, NJ: Educational Testing Service.

Dougherty, K. J. (1994). *The contradictory college: The conflicting origins, impacts, and futures of the community college.* Albany, NY: State University of New York Press.

Dougherty, K., & Kienzl, G. (2006, March). It's Not Enough to Get Through the Open Door: Inequalities by Social Background in Transfer from Community Colleges to Four-Year Colleges. *Teachers College Record, 108*(3), 452–487.

Gafford Muhammad, C. (2007, March). African Americans and college choice: The influence of family and school. *Urban Education, 42*(2), 185–190

Guy-Sheftall, B., & Bell Scott, P. (1989). Finding a way: Black women students and the academy. In C. S. Pearson (Ed.), *Educating the majority* (pp. 47–56). New York: Macmillan.

Hagedorn, L. S., Moon, H. S., Cypers, S., Maxwell, W. E., & Lester, J. (2006). Transfer between community colleges and 4-year colleges: The all-American game. *Community College Journal of Research and Practice, 30,* 223–242.

Hulbert, K. D., & Schuster, D. T. (1993). *Women's lives through time.* San Francisco, CA: Jossey-Bass.

Johnson, T. (2001). *Survival strategies of African American women in community colleges.* Unpublished doctoral dissertation, University of Texas at Austin.

Kisker, C. B. (2007). Creating and sustaining community college-university transfer partnerships. *Community College Review, 34*(4), 282–301.

Lewis, C. W., & Middleton, V. (2003). African Americans in community colleges: A review of research reported in the *Community College Journal of Research and Practice*: 1990–2000. *Community College Journal of Research and Practice, 27,* 787–798.

Lind, M. (1995). *The next American nation: The new nationalism and the fourth American revolution.* New York: Free Press.

McAtee, A. B., & Benshoff, J. M. (2006). Rural dislocated women in career transition: The importance of supports and strategies. *Community College Journal of Research and Practice, 30,* 697–714.

Melguizo, T. (2007). Latino and African-American students' transfer pathway to elite education in California. *Change, 39*(6), 52–55.

National Center for Education Statistics (NCES). (1999). *Digest of education statistics.* Washington, DC: U.S. Department of Education.

National Center for Education Statistics (NCES). (2007). *Digest of education statistics.* Washington, DC: U.S. Department of Education.

Pascarella, E., & Terenzini, P. T. (2005). *How college affects students: A third decade of research* (Vol. 2). San Francisco, CA: Jossey-Bass.

Provasnik, S., & Planty, M. (2008). *Community colleges: Special supplement to the condition of education 2008* (NCES 2008–033). Washington, DC: NCES, Institute of Education Sciences, U.S. Department of Education.

Rhoads, R. A., & J. R. Valadez. (1996). *Democracy, multiculturalism, and the community college.* New York: Garland Publishing.

Rifkin, T. (1996). Transfer and articulation policies: Implications for practice. In Rifkins, T. (Ed.), *Transfer and articulation: Improving policies to meet new needs* (pp. 77–85). New Directions for Community Colleges, No. 24. San Francisco: Jossey Bass.

Smith, M. H. (1993). *Family characteristics, social capital, and college attendance.* Digital Dissertations 505646. University of Florida, Gainesville.

Solorzano, D. G. (1995). The doctoral production and baccalaureate origins of African Americans in the sciences and engineering. *The Journal of Negro Education, 64,* 660–620.

Tidball, M. E. (1986). Baccalaureate origins of recent natural science doctorates. *Journal of Higher Education, 57*(6), 606–620.

Tidball, M. E., Smith, D. G., Tidball, C. S., & Wolf-Wendel, L. (1999). *Taking women seriously: Lessons and legacies for educating the majority.* Phoenix, AZ: Oryx Press.

Townsend, B. K., & Wilson, K. B. (2006). The transfer mission: Tried and true, but troubled? *New Directions for Community Colleges, 136,* 33–41.

U.S. Department of Education, National Center for Education Statistics (NCES). *Digest of Education Statistics, 2006* (NCES 2007–017), table 205, and NCES. (2003). *Digest of Education Statistics, 2002* (NCES 2003–061), table 207; data from U.S. Department of Education, NCES, 1976 and 1980 Higher Education General Information Survey (HEGIS), "Fall Enrollment in Colleges and Universities" surveys; and Integrated Postsecondary Education Data System, "Fall Enrollment Survey" (IPEDS-EF:00 and 95), and Spring 2001 and 2006.

Valadez, J. (1993, Winter). Cultural capital and its impact on the aspirations of non-traditional community college students. *Community College Review, 21*(3), 33–47.

Walpole, M. (2008, May). Emerging from the pipeline: African American students, socioeconomic status, and college experiences and outcomes. *Research in Higher Education, 49*(3), 237–255.

Wolf, L. E. (1995). *Models of excellence: The baccalaureate origins of successful European American women and Latinas.* Doctoral dissertation, Claremont Graduate School, Claremont, CA.

Wolf-Wendel, L. E. (1998). Models of excellence: The baccalaureate origins of successful European American women, African American women, and Latinas. *Journal of Higher Education, 69*, 141–187.

APPENDIX

LIST OF INDEPENDENT VARIABLES USED IN THE PRESENT ANALYSIS

Variable	*Code*
Father's education level Mother's education level	1 = Less Than HS 2 = HS 3 = College 4 = Masters, Professional 5 = Ph.D.
Gender	1 = Male 2 = Female
Junior College Attend	1 = Two-Year 0 = Four-Year
Age	25–60
Time in College Entry–Ph.D.	Total Time Enrolled in College From First Undergraduate Entrance to Receipt of First Doctorate
Respondent's Race/Ethnicity	1 = American Indian 2 = Asian 3 = Black 4 = Hispanic

	5 = White
	6 = Other/Multi
Respondent's Education Debt	1 = Less Than $10,000
	2 = Less Than $20,000
	3 = Less Than $30,000
	4 = $30,000 or More
B.A. Carnegie Classification	11 = "Research I"
M.A. Carnegie Classification	12 = "Research II"
Ph.D. Carnegie Classification	13 = "Doctoral I"

Variable	*Code*
	14 = "Doctoral II"
	21 = "Master's I"
	22 = "Master's II"
	31 = "Baccalaureate I"
	32 = "Baccalaureate II"
	40 = Associate of Arts
	51–59 = Specialized Institutions
	60 = Tribal College
Institutional Type	Research Colleges/Universities
	Doctoral-Granting Institutions
	Recoded:
B.A. Carnegie Classification	Research I/II
M.A. Carnegie Classification	Doctoral I/II
Ph.D. Carnegie Classification	Masters I/II
	Medical
H = Historically b = Black College/University Awarded First Baccalaureate (recode: H = 1, Blank = 2) B.A., M.A. Ph.D.	1 = Historically Black College/University Awarded First Baccalaureate (recode: H = 1, Blank = 0)
Combined Parents' Education Level	1 = Less Than HS
	2 = HS
	3 = College
	4 = Master's Professional
	5 = Ph.D.
Primary Source of Support	1 = Personal
	2 = University
Secondary Source of Support	3 = Federal
	4 = Awards
	5 = Other

8

A LOOK BACK AND A LOOK AHEAD

How to Navigate the Doctoral Degree Process Successfully

Benita J. Barnes

Nationally, nearly 50% of all doctoral students drop out of their degree programs before completion (Golde, 2000; Lovitts, 2001; Nettles & Millett, 2006), and approximately one out of five drops out after receiving candidacy (Peters, 1997). This problem is even more critical among students of color because they are already severely underrepresented in graduate school relative to their population in the United States (Johnson, 1996), and their attrition rate tops the 50% mark (Lovitts, 2001). One possible explanation for why so many students drop out of their doctoral programs could be that there are often no clear road maps for how to obtain a doctoral degree.

The doctoral education process can be both complex and convoluted, which has the potential to make any doctoral student feel more like a rat trying to make her way through a maze than a student trying to become a steward of her discipline. Feeling like a rat in a maze is enough to make anyone dizzy, despondent, and disenfranchised. However, these feelings can be more salient and detrimental to women and students of color because they often do not have the proper tools or resources to help them navigate their way through the contours of the maze (Hinchey & Kimmel, 2000; Patton & Harper, 2003). Although research to increase our understanding of the doctoral degree process for women and people of color has multiplied dramatically over the past decade (Austin, 2002), very little empirical research has been designed to lay out a road map of how to get through the graduate education process, or the doctoral degree maze (Hinchey & Kimmel, 2000).

The purpose of this autoethnography is twofold. First, it is to reflect on some of the experiences I encountered as an African American woman during my doctoral degree process and to share how I learned to navigate, manipulate, and orchestrate my way out of the doctoral degree maze. Second, it is to share my perspective as a faculty member about what I believe African American women need to do to earn their doctoral degrees. Beyond my personal experiences, I have an intellectual passion for both the student-mentee and the faculty-mentoring side of the doctoral process. Both facets of the process have been the center of my scholarly work for nearly a decade. As such, this autoethnography merges my student and faculty experiences with the scholarly work about which I have written and on which I reflected on for quite some time. It is my utmost hope that these reflections are of use to doctoral candidates and faculty alike.

Literature Review

Stages of the Doctoral Degree Process

The doctoral degree process can be divided into three stages—the beginning, the middle, and the end (Baird, 1995; Council of Graduate Schools [CGS], 1990). The beginning stage generally consists of year one and possibly the first part of year two. It is during this first stage that doctoral students become acquainted with the language and approach of the field, become familiar with people and the emphases of the program, get to know a group of their peers, find an adviser, and obtain funding (Baird, 1995). The middle stage of the doctoral degree process typically extends from year two until the student completes all of his or her course work. It is during this stage of the process that students usually master the language and habits of mind of their discipline, identify their intellectual and professional interests, select their committee members, and prepare for their comprehensive exams (Baird, 1995). The end or final stage of the doctoral program is typically called the dissertation stage. Students enter this stage after completing all other degree requirements and are considered ABD ("all but dissertation" or, more colloquially, "all but done"). It is during this final stage of the doctoral degree process that students are expected to conduct and defend an original piece of research (CGS, 1990). Although all of these stages appear to be very straightforward and easy to follow, what the stages fail to reveal are the political problems that can make the journey more difficult, if not impossible. For example, selecting a committee can involve extensive negotiation with institutional political ramifications that can have an impact on a student's degree progression. In addition, financial concerns and even simple matters of life occur, hindering, and in many cases foreclosing, degree completion.

Research on Graduate Students of Color

Persistence. Within the body of literature on doctoral education, several research streams have emerged relevant to the issue of underrepresented ethnic groups, particularly African Americans, in graduate school. One stream of research has focused on factors that influence students of color to persist in their graduate programs. The literature on persistence (Hamilton, 1998; King & Chepyator-Thomas, 1996; Thweatt-McCoy, 1998) suggests the student's individual commitment, earlier academic preparation, financial assistance, faculty mentoring, and institutional support programs during matriculation in graduate school heavily influence their graduate school success.

Satisfaction and success. A second stream of research that has received recent attention has centered on student satisfaction and success (DeBord & Millner, 1993; Ellis, 2001; Matthews & Jackson, 1991; Nettles, 1990). Research findings in this area of study suggest that satisfaction at the graduate level for students of color is linked to the amount of interaction students have with their peers and faculty, how integrated they are into their academic departments, and their overall involvement in the campus community.

In my own work, I have examined factors that lead to doctoral students' achievement outcomes. Barnes (2004) conducted a quantitative study that sought to understand the impact of various factors—personal persistence attributes, social interaction skills, university support structures, and adviser relationships—on doctoral students' success. The most significant thing I learned from this study was that the relationship a student had with her adviser had the highest impact on her achievement outcomes. This finding is well supported by previous research examining the importance of the adviser-advisee relationship (Baird, 1995; Lovitts, 2001; Nettles & Millet, 2006).

I have also found student interactions with peers to be a strong influence on student satisfaction and outcomes (Barnes, 2001). This research project, my first as a doctoral student, was qualitative and was designed to understand how African American women who attended either a historically Black college or university (HBCU) or a predominantly White institution (PWI) as undergraduates learned to navigate their way through the doctoral degree process at a PWI. One of the most intriguing things I learned from this study was that the students who had attended HBCUs as undergraduates fared much better academically and socially than did their peers who had attended PWIs as undergraduates. The women who had attended HBCUs as undergraduates engaged more frequently with their peers and were much more integrated into their departments. For example, one woman spoke about how she would attend a local pub after class (even though she personally did not drink) in an effort to interact socially with her classmates. She also talked about how all of her classmates, both female and male, attended her baby shower that was sponsored by her department. Another woman who had attended an HBCU talked about how she made it a point to attend all of the brown bag meetings and colloquiums that her department sponsored so she would always be in the know.

Sadly, the women who had attended PWIs as undergraduates had no such stories to tell about their doctoral experiences because they did not interact with their peers on a social or academic level outside the classroom. As undergraduates, these women experienced their education on the margins, and as doctoral students, they were still isolating themselves academically and socially from both their departments and their peers. It was as if the only place they knew where to live their academic lives was on the margins. By not experiencing their academic journeys from the middle (like their peers who attended HBCUs as undergraduates), and by not becoming integrated into their departments, these women suffered more delays and setbacks to their degree completion.

Results from this study support the ideas advanced by Tinto (1993) regarding the importance of doctoral students' academic and social integration. Clearly, the students who were more academically and socially integrated (those who had attended HBCUs) experienced more satisfaction and success in their doctoral programs than did their peers who had attended

PWIs as undergraduates. Previous research on doctoral student socialization suggests that students who are not properly integrated or socialized during the doctoral degree process will often be less satisfied with their doctoral degree experience and take longer to complete their degrees, if they complete them at all (Lovitts, 2001).

Social support and mentoring. A third stream of research that has emerged from the field has focused on social support and mentoring (Blackwell, 1983; Faison, 1996; White, 1995; Willie, Grady, & Hope, 1991). Findings from studies in this area indicate that mentoring is a crucial part of the graduate student experience, and students who have mentors reported higher levels of satisfaction with their graduate school experiences than did those without mentors. Some graduate education pundits have argued that mentoring is so important in graduate education that it is at the heart of the graduate school experience (Cusanovich & Gilliland, 1991).

In spite of the plethora of literature supporting the notion that advisers play a critical role in the academic success of their doctoral advisees (Cheatham & Phelps, 1995; Holland, 1998; Lovitts, 2001; Lyons, Scroggins, & Rule, 1990), there is a paucity of research examining this phenomenon from the advisers' perspectives (see Knox, Schlosser, Pruitt, & Hill, 2006, for an exception). Therefore, my dissertation research (Barnes, in press) examined the adviser-advisee relationship from the perspectives of 25 exemplary advisers. Two of the most noteworthy things I learned from this study are what advisers expect from their advisees and what dynamics most influence how advisers work with their advisees. First, with regard to expectations, the four most critical expectations advisers have of their advisees are that they will be committed to the doctoral degree process, they will have integrity, they will make consistent degree progress, and they will be good department and disciplinary citizens. The single greatest influence that affected how an adviser worked with her advisee was the advisee herself. What the advisee brings to the relationship in terms of her attitude, dedication, and personality best determines how her adviser will interact with her.

Professional socialization. A fourth, although limited, stream of research has focused on the student socialization process. To understand the differences between the socialization process for minority and majority women doctoral students, Turner and Thompson (1993) interviewed 37 minority doctoral women students and 25 majority women doctoral students. They used a semistructured questionnaire as a guide to examine the process of personal and professional development of respondents. Students were asked to describe the kinds of relationships they had with other students and faculty, and the range and types of opportunities they had for acquiring professional values and skills inside and outside the classroom. They identified student perceptions on four points from the interview data: (a) the institution's recruitment process; (b) departmental opportunities for apprenticeship and mentoring experiences; (c) a cooperative or competitive departmental environment; and (d) racial and gender discrimination in their department. Their findings showed that minority women had fewer opportunities for professional socialization experiences, less mentoring, fewer apprenticeship experiences, and fewer networks within their departments. Moreover, Sulé (in press) found that instead of professional socialization into the field, Black women doctoral candidates were encouraged to assume subordinated roles based on their race and gender. In this vein they were organizationally acculturated within an academic caste system that marginalized their work.

In summary, the last two decades have seen a surge in research on students of color in graduate school in an effort to understand what factors contribute to their academic success. Based on a review of the literature, four research themes emerged as central points of focus: persistence, social support and mentoring, student satisfaction and success, and student socialization process. Although these studies have been very useful in helping us understand which factors have an impact on the success of doctoral students of color, very few if any of these studies have been useful in helping us understand how doctoral students navigate their way through the doctoral degree process.

Autoethnography as a Research Approach

Ethnography is a branch of the field of anthropology that focuses on the analysis of culture. In traditional ethnography, the researcher inserts himself or herself in the field and studies "the other." At the same time, and in direct tension, it is the goal of the traditional ethnographer "to remove the researcher's influence from the study and the presentation" (Davis, 2005, p. 533). Autoethnography is an extension of ethnography in which the focus is on the researcher's experience. In autoethnographic research, the purpose of the study is to explore a social phenomenon present in the researcher's own group using his or her personal experience with that phenomenon (Davis,

2005). Autoethnographic research can take the form of poetry, short stories, fiction, photographic essays, personal essays, journals, and social science prose (Davis, 2005; Ellis & Bochner, 2000).

This particular autoethnographic study falls under the category of personal narrative. In personal narratives, the researcher takes on the dual identities of academic and personal selves. From the side of the personal self, stories are told about some aspects of an experience in daily life. The academic self, then, situates the personal narrative within the broader social context and scholarship (Ellis & Bochner, 2000). In this personal narrative, I write about the doctoral experience from two of my own personal perspectives. The first is a reflection of my own experience as a doctoral student. The second is from my current lens as a faculty member who is responsible for advising doctoral students. Data for this analysis come from my journal entries, e-mails, and recollections.

Insights From My Doctoral Experience

I began my doctoral program in the fall of 2000. My passion for and dedication to obtaining my doctorate knew no boundaries. I had finally found something to which I could truly commit. My commitment to obtaining my doctoral degree was stronger than any commitments I had been able to make to anything or anyone else before, including several marriage proposals. In fact, my commitment to my doctoral program was so strong, I purchased a gold band and wore it on the ring finger of my left hand. It was there to remind me that regardless of how tough the process was or how ugly the situation turned, I was in it for the long haul and I would not quit. The ring also served as homage to the Black women who came before me. I understood that I had not arrived at the doctoral level due to my own goodness and intelligences. Instead, I had gotten there by walking across the backs and climbing on the shoulders of the Black women (as well as other women and some men) who came before me. I also knew that many of those Black women had been much more intelligent, far more capable, and definitely more deserving than I of a doctoral degree, but due to their lot in life they did not have the opportunity to obtain one. So it was also in their honor and in their memory that I donned the ring and was prepared to move full speed ahead.

The biggest mistake I made at the start of my doctoral program was setting too high expectations of the program faculty. More specifically, I (mistakenly) thought the faculty would embrace my being in the program as strongly as I had embraced being in the program. I thought that the faculty would automatically mentor me, groom me, and bring me into the "fold" just because *they* were fortunate enough to have *me* in their program. Finally, I thought that by admitting me into the doctoral program, the faculty were publicly declaring their unwavering pledge to see me through the program. I found out rather quickly, however, that this was less than true. From my perspective, the faculty did not appear to be nearly as excited to have me in the program as I was to be in the program. Nor did they seem nearly as interested in mentoring me, grooming me, or bringing me into the fold as I was for them to do so. Finally, they did not seem nearly as committed to seeing me graduate from the program as I was to graduate from the program. These early disappointments made me realize that if I were going to be successful, I needed to knuckle down and be willing to become the author of my own fate and the finisher of my own story.

I learned two key lessons by the end of my first year that allowed me to navigate the rest of my doctoral degree training successfully. The first was that I had to develop networks and allies outside my department. The second was that I needed to be actively engaged in research projects.

When I was admitted to my doctoral program, I was offered a three-year assistantship in my department as the coordinator of an undergraduate leadership course. Although there was nothing inherently wrong with doing administrative work, administration was not the area in which I was looking to hone my skills. Therefore, I knew early on that I did not want to continue in that position after my first year; I wanted a research position. After having several difficult conversations with the program administration regarding my not wanting to return to my administrative position for a second year, it was made clear to me that if I was not willing to accept what the department had to offer I would be left to find my own assistantship, which I was told would be almost impossible. I decided to bear the challenge, and I told my supervisor that I would not be returning to my assistantship for a second year. Although having the academic year end without knowing where or if I would have an assistantship the following fall was scary and uncomfortable, I knew that going in search of a research assistantship would be worth the discomfort. After sending numerous e-mails to everyone from the vice president of student affairs to the dean of the graduate school, I finally secured two quarter-time research assistantships. One of the positions was with the vice president for student affairs and the other was with the associate dean for student affairs in the graduate school. In hindsight, striking out on my own was one of the best decisions I could have made. Although I no longer had an assistantship connected to my department, which isolated me from my faculty and peers, the new assistantships enabled me to enlarge my support networks to include people I would not have known otherwise. Both the vice president for student affairs and the associate dean for student affairs in the graduate school served as my mentors, advocated on my behalf, wrote letters of recommendation, and made certain that I had financial support throughout the remainder of my doctoral program.

The second way I increased my opportunities to broaden my social networks was by becoming involved in student government. Student involvement has long been linked to retention and satisfaction at the undergraduate level (Astin, 1984; Tinto, 1993); however, Gardner and Barnes (2007) found that involvement at the graduate level contributes to students' socialization and networking opportunities. My involvement in the Council of Graduate Students (COGS) enabled me to increase my networks across campus because I sat on numerous university-wide committees and was able to develop professional relationships with top-level administrators and faculty from other departments and disciplines. I am convinced that one reason I received the number of fellowships I did was because I was known throughout the campus. Therefore, based on my experience, I encourage graduate students, particularly African American women who can find the time, to gain campus visibility by getting involved with various department or university-wide committees. I found that university officials wanted graduate students, particularly women and students of color, to serve on committees and in other official capacities. At the very least, even part-time students can and should take the opportunity to meet informally with faculty and administrators who share commonalities—especially research interests. The onus is on the doctoral students to make themselves visible. The truth of the matter is, no one is trying to figure out that they exist on campus. Therefore, they have to make their existence known, and the best way for them to do that is by becoming visible and active in a public way. Even women who have full-time work and parenting commitments can gain visibility within their departments by being "good" students, being supportive of fellow class-mates, making the time to meet with key faculty, and attending departmental functions whenever possible.

Overall, developing networks and allies helped me navigate the doctoral degree process in two ways. First, the administrators who gave me the research assistantships became truly invested in me—they became my mentors. As a result, they served as listening ears anytime I broached them about a problem, situation, or concern I was having. They always advised me of multiple ways to handle any particular situation, and they helped me think through the pros and cons of all of my options. In addition, both of them, but particularly the associate graduate dean for student affairs, were always willing to guide me around academic/professional minefields and to help me understand the nature of the academy, which contributed to my socialization into the academic profession (Austin & McDaniels, 2006). Second, my involvement with COGS allowed me to sit on a variety of committees, which gave me insight into the overall university process and introduced me to faculty from other disciplines who were willing to become my cheerleaders and supporters throughout my doctoral program.

During doctoral training, students should learn how to discover, integrate, and apply knowledge, as well as disseminate and communicate it (Katz, 1997). All of these skills are part of the research process in general and the dissertation process in particular. Therefore, African American doctoral students need to have ample opportunities not only to learn these skills but also to practice them before embarking on their dissertation research. Research has shown that doctoral students who engage in faculty-directed research that culminates in scholarly publications are better prepared for the rigorous inquiry needed to complete the dissertation (Brewer, Douglas, Facer, & O'Toole, 1999). After all, the best way to learn to do research is by conducting research (Lincoln, 2006). However, many students in professional fields such as education and social work often do not have the opportunity to be involved in research projects before undertaking their dissertation research. This lack of opportunity and experience can increase the amount of time students spend lingering in limbo once they become ABD (Lovitts, 2008).

Becoming a "scholar" was my intent when I entered my doctoral program. Therefore, as I alluded to earlier, being engaged in research projects was of high importance to me. Even after I had secured two research-focused assistantships, I was still interested in becoming part of a faculty research team. I had two particular motivations for joining a faculty research team rather than just being satisfied with my two research assistantships. My first motivation was that I wanted to be a part of a group of people who were working on the same research project so that I could have people to collaborate with and learn from, which is integral to the professional socialization of graduate students (Austin & McDaniels, 2006). My second motivation was my belief that by working with a faculty member on his or her research, I would have a better chance of getting data to present at conferences and to publish. I was right on both counts.

Getting connected with a faculty-sponsored research project was not easy. I had to beat the pavement and talk with a number of faculty members both inside and outside my department about the type of research they were conducting and ask if I could work with them as a volunteer. I finally connected with one of the professors outside of my doctoral program with whom I had taken a number of measurement and statistic courses. The research knowledge I gained from both my research assistantships and the faculty research project was invaluable and contributed immensely to my being prepared to conduct dissertation research. For example, while working on the graduate school's research project, I saw the numerous ways in which a research project could get delayed when one has to depend on other sources or offices for information. I also learned from working on that research project the importance of piloting the survey instrument or interview protocol. In addition, working on a professor's research team taught me how to work through unanticipated research design issues and data collection problems that cropped up during the research process. Finally, by being responsible for writing the results or portions of the results from my various research projects, I got a firsthand glimpse of how iterative the writing process actually is.

Collectively, these experiences helped me develop the habits of mind that are essential to higher education and that are integral to the socialization of doctoral students. Because of the experience I gained from working on other research projects, by the time I was ready to undertake my own research project, I was realistic about how long the research process (particularly data collection and analysis) can take. Moreover, I was better able to solve research design issues, and I understood that writing a dissertation is an iterative process. By the time I reached the dissertation stage of the doctoral degree process, I was well prepared to transition into what Gardner (2008) and Lovitts (2005, 2008) call an independent researcher.

Dissertation research can be one of the most difficult and mystifying aspects of the doctoral degree process. Therefore, being socialized to the art and science of conducting research before embarking on your own dissertation project is a great advantage and prepares you to become an independent researcher (Gardner, 2008; Lovitts, 2008). Although students may take a variety of courses that prepare them theoretically to conduct independent empirical research, this academic training is not always sufficient to teach them how to deal with the many unanticipated problems that may emerge during the research process. In addition, conducting your own research, beyond class assignments, helps you to locate your authentic academic writing voice. Therefore, there is no substitute for gaining hands-on research experience before undertaking your own dissertation project. The practical experience gained from conducting research takes the mystery out of "doing" research, and it can make the difference between having the skills, knowledge, and ability to complete the dissertation and not.

Regardless of their full- or part-time status, familial or work commitments, doctoral students can work actively toward becoming more scholarly. One small exercise you can tackle with minimal guidance is the book review. Colleges and universities are full of pamphlets from booksellers advertising new titles. Pick something of interest. Write the publisher and ask for a review copy, find a journal with an interest in such a book, and then write a summary that includes your insights. Use previous reviews as a guide. If you are more ambitious, write a review essay synthesizing two or more scholarly works together. Moreover, in your talks with faculty, find out what they are working on and ask if you may help, perhaps just by writing a small section of the literature review. In doing so you will be able to watch the research process unfold, albeit from the sidelines, which will help demystify the process.

Insights From My Faculty Experience

Looking at doctoral education from a faculty perspective is definitely a different lens through which to view the doctoral degree process. Whereas when I was a doctoral student I thought it was critical for me to find others who were willing to invest in me and my success, as a faculty member, I see that it is even more important for doctoral students to be willing to invest in themselves. Since entering the professoriate in the fall of 2005, I have come to believe that there are two critical ways in which doctoral students need to invest in themselves. The first is by committing themselves to going through the *process*. Although there is no single definition of the *process*, one way I think about it is in terms of the intellectual, psychological, and emotional changes/development/growth one has to go through and endure to earn the doctoral degree (Green, 1997). Earning a doctorate is a transformational procedure, and with it comes ambiguity, uncertainty, and dissonances. However, being open to and expecting a metamorphosis is key to survival. As a faculty member, I often see students who are resistant to their own metamorphosis. These students, for example, resist struggling through writing projects necessary for them to become what Baxter-Magolda (1998) calls "self-authored." According to Baxter-Magolda, self-authorship "requires a sense of identity through which individuals perceive themselves as capable of knowledge construction" (p. 41). Instead, they are looking for a formulaic way of getting through the writing process, and they want their professors to provide them with the formula. This type of behavior or mind-set is damaging and often leads to frustration and a lack of preparedness to conduct dissertation research (Lovitts, 2008).

The other way I have begun to think about the *process* since becoming a faculty member is the second way I believe doctoral students need to invest in themselves, and that is by owning their own process. In this context, the term *process* means the formal procedures that often accompany earning a doctorate. Every institution has its own set of academic milestones (prelims, comps, qualifying exams, proposal defense, etc.) that students must achieve to graduate. In addition, as students approach and conquer each academic milestone, they usually must file official paperwork. Therefore, I recommend that doctoral students take the time early in their program to familiarize themselves with the details of the procedures associated with each milestone and to learn what forms they must file. Familiarization with both steps helps demystify the process by allowing students to ask questions in advance. It also gives them a better sense of how to approach and prepare to conquer each milestone.

A broad definition of professional socialization is "the process of transforming a human being into a self who possesses a sense of identity and is endowed with appropriate attitudes, values, and ways of thinking, and with other personal yet social attributes" (Coombs, 1978, p. 14). The socialization process at the doctoral level involves becoming socialized to being a doctoral student as well as being socialized into one's future profession (Austin & McDaniels, 2006; Golde, 1998). Therefore, both committing to the process and owning the process as described here are integral to becoming successfully socialized as a graduate student.

As a doctoral student, I often wondered if the students who were being mentored were getting mentored because they were good students, or if it was the mentoring these students were receiving that made them good students. As a faculty member, I believe it is primarily the former. "Good" students are those who enter their programs demonstrating they have intellectual curiosity, they are willing to work hard, and they are interested in becoming professionally engaged, and, as a result, they are the ones whom faculty members gravitate to and in whom faculty are willing to invest (Hilmer & Hilmer, 2007). My conjecture is also supported by the results of the Green and Bauer (1995) study on who gets mentored in graduate school. They found that the students who were mentored were also the ones who showed a promise to perform at the beginning of their doctoral program.

Mentoring in the context of graduate education has been described as "a process that provides individuals with support and protection during their graduate training" (Frierson, 1997, p. 2). A number of studies suggest that mentoring relationships between faculty and graduate students are essential to graduate school success (Luna & Cullen, 1998; Lyons et al., 1990; Waldeck, Orrego, Plax, & Kearney, 1997). Furthermore, some graduate education pundits have argued that mentoring is so important in graduate education that it is at the heart of the experience (Cusanovich & Gilliland, 1991; Phillips, 1979).

As a faculty member, the number of responsibilities vying for my time and attention are numerous (teaching, research, and service), so I have to be very judicious about how I invest my time and in whom I invest it, and (unfortunately) this judicious process includes mentoring doctoral students. Thus, the only students I can afford to mentor are those whom I deem "mentorable." Based on my personal definition, mentorable students are those who are eager to learn, willing to go the extra mile, willing to push their own comfort levels to grow, value their doctoral educational experience, and are humble and moldable. The literature on graduate education suggests that being mentored is important to all doctoral students' success, but that it is particularly important for the success of women and students of color (Nettles, 1990; Turner & Thompson, 1993). Therefore, women and students of color must be very intentional about developing and displaying mentorable characteristics.

Related to mentoring is advising. A growing body of graduate education literature speaks to the important role that advisers play in the success of their doctoral students (Austin, 2002; Lovitts, 2001). As a faculty member, if there is a single piece of advice I would give to any doctoral student, but particularly to other African American women, it would be to develop an effective and authentic relationship with the person who is your doctoral adviser. Your adviser—just by the nature of his or her position—can influence many aspects of your doctoral degree experience, such as your research opportunities, conference participation, publication possibilities, and fellowship options (Cheatham & Phelps, 1995). The ultimate type of relationship you can develop with your adviser is a mentor-mentee relationship, and the best way to do that is to show that you are mentorable as discussed above. However, for a number of reasons, your relationship with your adviser may not develop into a mentor-mentee relationship. Be that as it may, you still need to have an excellent and effective working relationship with him or her because your adviser will be the principal person who guides you through your plan of study as well as the often-harrowing dissertation process. Furthermore, and perhaps more important, your adviser will be the one person from whom everyone, from the fellowship committee to future employers, will expect to receive a letter of recommendation. Therefore, it is essential that your adviser has a good perspective on who you are.

As an adviser myself, I see three things that set the foundation for my developing an effective relationship with my advisees (even if I am serving more as an adviser than a mentor). First, there must be honesty. For me to have an authentic relationship with my advisees, I have to be able to be honest with them, or the relationship is not going to work well. Being honest with my advisees entails many things, but one of the most important is that I have to be able to tell them (without their falling apart or changing advisers) when they are not progressing or when they are doing things that are destructive to their success. For example, I recently had an advisee who did not complete all of her course assignments by the end of fall semester for one of the core doctoral courses, so she was given an incomplete for the course.

I was livid when I found out that she was assigned an incomplete because I knew that, by her not completing the course during the semester in which she had enrolled, she could be dismissed from the program at the end of spring semester for not making "adequate" progress. Therefore, when I met with her at the beginning of spring semester, I "read her the riot act" about how she was jeopardizing her standing and reputation in the program. Suffice it to say that my interaction with my advisee that day was not pretty, but it was necessary. It was necessary because I was genuinely angered by her actions, or inaction. I had to let her know it, and I had to be able to do so in a manner that was authentic for me. As a result of that interaction, I believe we both walked away from the incident understanding each other better and appreciating each other more. Today my relationship with that student is even stronger because I am able to be my authentic self with her. Second, my advisees have to respect my time. This primarily includes keeping scheduled appointments, coming to meetings prepared, following up and through with agreed-upon assignments, and being responsive. Finally, my advisees must be serious about earning their doctoral degrees and not just be in the program because they want a credential. Their seriousness is made most evident by their willingness to work hard and their commitment to the process.

I think one of the biggest secrets to completing a doctorate is knowing how to develop and sustain relationships with people, and the relationship with your doctoral adviser is one of the most important relationships you will have to sustain. Although some advisers make developing a relationship with them easier than do others, regardless of how easy or difficult developing the relationship may be, you owe it to yourself to do so (Barnes, in press). After all, it could spell the difference between completing your degree and not completing it.

Concluding Thoughts

The purpose of this chapter was to offer insights from my own doctoral education experience and my faculty experience to provide a road map for African American women to navigate their way successfully through the doctoral degree maze. Therefore, to that end, what follows are suggestions culled from both perspectives.

First, although you alone can earn your doctorate, you cannot earn your doctoral degree alone. Therefore, building wide circles of faculty and peer networks is going to be critical to your academic success.

Second, a big part of being successful in graduate school is having the right attitude about the process. Therefore, "own" your process. Find meaning and value in all of your experiences, the good and the not so good. Remember, earning a doctoral degree is an intellectually transformational process; therefore, do not fight the transformation. Related to owning the process from an intellectual perspective, you also need to own the process from a programmatic perspective. Learn what "hoops" your degree program entails well before you have to jump through them. Find out what paperwork needs to be managed at every stage of the process and know whose signatures are required and with whom the paperwork needs to be filed. Let the doctoral degree process be something you control, not something that controls you.

Third, be mentorable. One of the best ways to navigate the doctoral degree process is by having a navigator. Your navigator (more commonly known as your mentor) will be able to walk you around academic minefields and protect you from other unseen dangers. However, to attract a mentor, you must be seen as mentorable, which includes being humble and moldable. No one wants a mentee who is arrogant and obstinate.

Fourth, develop an effective relationship with your adviser whether or not that person serves as your mentor. Although most advisers probably have some philosophical principles that guide their advising practice, few, if any, have any professional training on how to be a doctoral adviser. As a result, your adviser will probably advise you based on what he or she perceives your needs to be. Therefore, be upfront about what you need from your adviser and find out what he or she expects from you. Present yourself as motivated, intellectually curious, and committed to getting the degree. Above all, demonstrate personal and professional integrity. In a nutshell, knowing how to navigate the doctoral degree process successfully is really about knowing how to manage processes and how to build and sustain relationships with people.

References

Astin, A. W. (1984). Student involvement: A developmental theory for higher education. *Journal of College Student Personnel, 25,* 297–308.

Austin, A. E. (2002). Preparing the next generation of faculty: Graduate school as socialization to academic career. *Journal of Higher Education, 73*(1), 94–122.

Austin, A. E., & McDaniels, M. (2006). Preparing the professoriate of the future: Graduate student socialization for faculty roles. *Higher Education: Handbook of Theory and Research, 21,* 397–456.

Baird, L. L. (1995). Helping graduate students: A graduate adviser's view. In A. S. Pruitt-Logan & P. D. Isaac (Eds.), *Student services for the changing graduate student population* (pp. 25–32). New Directions for Student Services, No. 72. San Francisco, CA: Jossey-Bass.

Barnes, B. J. (2001). *African American graduate student success: Is there a difference in the role historically Black and predominantly White undergraduate institutions play?* Unpublished manuscript, Michigan State University, East Lansing.

Barnes, B. J. (2004, November) *Doctoral students' success: Factors that lead to achievement outcomes.* Paper presented at the annual meeting of the Association for the Study of Higher Education, Kansas City, MO.

Barnes, B. J. (in press). The nature of exemplary adviser's expectations and the ways they may influence doctoral persistence. *Journal of College Student Retention: Research, Theory & Practice.*

Baxter-Magolda, M. B. (1998). Developing self-authorship in graduate school. In M. S. Anderson (Ed.), *The experience of being in graduate school: An exploration,* (pp. 41–54). New Directions for Higher Education, No. 101. San Francisco, CA: Jossey-Bass

Blackwell, J. E. (1983). *Networking and mentoring: A study of cross-generational experiences of Blacks in graduate and professional school* (Research Report). Atlanta, GA: Southern Educational Foundation.

Brewer, G. A., Douglas, J. W., Facer, R. L, II, & O'Toole, L. J., Jr. (1999). Determinants of graduate research productivity in doctoral programs of public administration. *Public Administration Review, 59*(5), 373–382.

Cheatham, H. E., & Phelps, C. E. (1995). Promoting the development of graduate students of color. *New Directions for Student Services, 72,* 91

Coombs, R. H. (1978). *Mastering medicine.* New York: The Free Press.

Council of Graduate Schools (CGS). (1990). *Research student and supervisor: An approach to good supervisory practice.* Washington, DC: Author.

Cusanovich, M., & Gilliland, M. (1991). Mentoring: The faculty-graduate student relationship. *Communicator, 24* (6), 1–3.

Davis, S. D. (2005). Beyond technique: An autoethnographic exploration of how I learned to show love towards my father. *The Qualitative Report, 10*(3) 533–542. Retrieved October 22, 2006, from http://www.nova.edu/sss/QR/QR10–3/davis.pdf

DeBord, L. W., & Millner, S. M. (1993). Educational experiences of African American graduate students on a traditionally White campus: Succor, sociation, and success. *Equity & Excellence in Education, 26*(1), 60–71.

Ellis, C., & Bochner, A. P. (2000). Autoethnography, personal narrative, reflexivity: Researcher as subject. In N. K Denzin & Y. S. Lincoln (Eds.), *Handbook of qualitative research* (2nd ed., pp. 733–768). Thousand Oaks, CA: Sage Publications.

Ellis, E. M. (2001). The impact of race and gender on graduate school socialization, satisfaction with doctoral study, and commitment to degree completion. *Western Journal of Black Studies, 25*(1), 30–45.

Faison, J. J. (1996). *The next generation: The mentoring of African American graduate students on predominately white campuses* (ERIC Document Reproduction Service No. ED 401344).

Frierson, H. T., Jr. (Ed.). (1997). *Diversity in higher education: Mentoring and diversity in higher education* (Vol. 1). Greenwich, CT: JAI Press, Inc.

Gardner, S. K. (2008). "What's too much and what's too little?": The process of becoming an independent researcher in higher education. *Journal of Higher Education, 79*(3), 326–350.

Gardner, S. K., & Barnes, B. J. (2007). Graduate student involvement: Socialization for the professional role. *Journal of College Student Development, 48*(4), 1–19.

Golde, C. M. (1998). Beginning graduate school: Explaining first-year doctoral attrition. In M. S. Anderson (Ed.), *The experience of being in graduate school: An exploration* (pp. 55–64). New Directions for Higher Education, No. 101. San Francisco, CA: Jossey-Bass

Golde, C. M. (2000). Should I stay or should I go? Student descriptions of the doctoral attrition process. *Review of Higher Education, 23*(4) 199–228.

Green, K. E. (1997). Psychosocial factors affecting dissertation completion. In L. F. Goodchild, K. E. Green, E. L. Katz, & R. C. Kluever (Eds.), *Rethinking the dissertation process: Tackling personal and institutional obstacles* (pp. 57–64). New Directions for Higher Education, No. 99. San Francisco, CA: Jossey-Bass.

Green, S. G., & Bauer, T. N. (1995). Supervisory mentoring by advisers: Relationships with doctoral student potential, productivity, and commitment. *Personnel Psychology, 48*, 537–561.

Hamilton, C. A. (1998). *Factors that influenced the persistence of minority doctoral students at Northeastern Research University* (Doctoral dissertation, State University of New York at Albany, 1998). *Dissertation Abstracts International, 59*, 0627.

Hilmer, C. E., & Hilmer, M. J. (2007). On the relationship between the student-adviser match and early career research productivity for agricultural and resource economics Ph.D.s. *American Journal of Agricultural Economics, 89*(1), 162–175.

Hinchey, P., & Kimmel, I. (2000). *The graduate grind: A critical look at graduate education.* New York: Falmer Press.

Holland, J. W. (1998). Mentoring and the faculty development of African-American doctoral students. In H. T. Frierson Jr. (Ed.), *Diversity in higher education: Vol. 2. Examining protégé-mentor experiences* (pp. 17–40). Stamford, CT: JAI Press.

Johnson, I. (1996, Summer). Access and retention: Support programs for graduate and professional students. In I. H. Johnson & A. J. Ottens (Eds.), *Leveling the playing field: Promoting success for students of color* (pp. 53–64). New Directions for Student Services, No. 74. San Francisco, CA: Jossey-Bass.

Katz, E. L. (1997). Key players in the dissertation process. In L. F. Goodchild, K. E. Green, E. L Katz, & R. C. Kluever (Eds.), *Rethinking the dissertation process: Tackling personal and institutional obstacles* (pp. 5–16). New Directions for Higher Education, No. 99. San Francisco, CA: Jossey-Bass.

King, S. E., & Chepyator-Thomson, J. R. (1996). Factors affecting the enrollment and persistence of African American doctoral students. *The Physical Educator, 53,* 170–180.

Knox, S., Schlosser, L. Z., Pruitt, N. T., & Hill, C. E. (2006). A qualitative examination of graduate advising relationships: The adviser perspective. *The Counseling Psychologist, 34*(4), 489–518.

Lincoln, Y. S. (2006). Life under construction: Autoethnography of a researcher. *Higher Education: Handbook of Theory and Research, 21,* 1–38.

Lovitts, B. E. (2001). *Leaving the ivory tower: The causes and consequences of departure from doctoral study.* Lanham, MD: Rowman & Littlefield.

Lovitts, B. E. (2005). Being a good course-taker is not enough: A theoretical perspective on the transition to independent research. *Studies in Higher Education, 30*(2), 137–154.

Lovitts, B. E. (2008). The transition to independent research: Who makes it, who doesn't and why? *Journal of Higher Education, 79*(3), 296–325.

Luna, G., & Cullen, D. L. (1998). Do graduate students need mentoring? *College Student Journal, 23*(3), 322–330.

Lyons, W., Scroggins, D., & Rule, P. B. (1990). The mentor in graduate education. *Studies in Higher Education, 15*(3), 277–285.

Matthews, W., & Jackson, K. W. (1991). Determinants of success for Black males and females in graduate and professional schools. In W. R. Allen, E. G. Epps, & N. Z. Haniff (Eds.), *College in Black and white: African American students in predominantly White and in historically Black public universities* (pp. 197–208). Albany, NY: State University of New York Press.

Nettles, M. T. (1990). Success in doctoral programs: Experiences of minority and White students. *American Journal of Education, 98*(4), 494–522.

Nettles, M. T., & Millett, C. M. (2006). *Three magic letters: Getting to Ph.D.* Baltimore, MD: The Johns Hopkins University Press.

Patton, L. D., & Harper, S. R. (2003). Mentoring relationship among African American women in graduate and professional schools. In M. F. Howard-Hamilton (Ed.), *Meeting the needs of African American women* (pp. 67–78). New Directions for Student Services, No. 104. San Francisco, CA: Jossey-Bass.

Peters, R. L. (1997). *Getting what you came for: The smart student's guide to earning a Master's or Ph.D* (2nd ed.). New York: Noonday Press.

Phillips, G. M. (1979). The peculiar intimacy of graduate study: A conservative view. *Communication Education, 28,* 339–345.

Sulé, T. V. (in press). Professional socialization, politicized raced and gendered experience and Black female graduate students: A Roadmap for structural transformation. In B. Bush, C. Gafford Muhammad, and W. Walpole (Eds.). *From diplomas to doctorates: The success of Black women in higher education and its implications for equal educational opportunities for all.* Sterling, VA: Stylus.

Thweatt-McCoy, V. (1998). *Experiences of African-American women in doctoral programs.* (Doctoral dissertation, Virginia Polytechnic Institute and State University, 1998). *Dissertation Abstracts International, 59,* 3374.

Tinto, V. (1993). *Leaving college: Rethinking the causes and cures of student attrition* (2nd ed.). Chicago, IL: The University of Chicago Press.

Turner, C. S. V., & Thompson, J. R. (1993). Socializing women doctoral students: Minority and majority experiences. *Review of Higher Education, 16,* 355–370.

Waldeck, J. H., Orrego, V. O., Plax, T. G., & Kearney, P. (1997*). Communication Quarterly, 45*(3), 93–109.

White, J. W. (1995). *Increasing the flow of Black Ph.D's: A comparison of Black doctoral fellows in a comprehensive support program with Black doctoral students without a comprehensive support program.* (Doctoral dissertation, University of Maryland College Park, 1995). *Dissertation Abstracts International, 56,* 3024.

Willie, C. V., Grady, M. K., & Hope, R. O. (1991). *African-Americans and the doctoral experience: Implications for policy.* New York: Teachers College Press.

This book presents research regarding factors that affect the educational process of African American women. The authors brilliantly illuminate the steadfastness of young Black women as they progress from high school through graduate school. The book's focus on lessons learned from successes and challenges will make the educational process much more manageable for future generations of African American women. The authors invited me to offer some insights for managing life beyond the classroom based on my own experience. Several clichés and popular sayings came to mind, such as "just do it," "never give up," and "to whom much is given, much is expected." Upon further reflection I discovered that the secret to my success, measured in longevity and productivity, is largely due to my continuing development as a whole person—not just a professional person.

One day at work I was feeling particularly overwhelmed and wishing with all my might that a day would miraculously expand to a 48-hour block of time when the phone rang. It was an odd call because it was my mother, and she, as a rule, did not call me at work. When the panic I felt subsided, I could hear her say emphatically, "Wonder Woman only exists in the movies, and even there she is a fictional character!" This is probably my greatest life lesson because it gives me a reality check on my place in the universe. I abandoned my super heroine alter ego and embraced the reality that I cannot do everything. This is liberating to me even now because it frees me to focus my energy on the things that I can do.

During my elementary school years, there was an eagerly anticipated ritual of identifying the students who would be promoted to the next grade. This notion of promotion took on a whole new meaning when I entered the academy as a tenure-track assistant professor. I busied myself as I had been socialized to do (e.g., autonomy in work, competitive productivity, protecting intellectual capital, survival of the fittest, etc.). I remember having strong feelings of empathy for gerbils because I felt that I was running on a wheel in a cage. The worst part of my new career was feeling all alone in my struggle, feeling isolated and ill equipped to succeed. In conversations with some of my peers at other institutions, I discovered that I could write my story, regarding fitting in as an African American woman, and the same story would fit my sisters elsewhere in the country. We discovered "strength in numbers" so to speak and formed what I can only describe as a family. There are five of us whom I think of as a nuclear professional family, and over the years we have supported each other collectively in both professional and personal matters. We have spent countless hours and dollars on telephone calls that come late in the night, early in the morning, or sometimes in the middle of the day! It is comforting to be part of an intimate group of mutual support. I urge those of you who are starting your careers, whatever the field, to find African American women with whom you can relate as soul mates. Not everyone will fit that criterion, but it is very important to know that African American women, as a group, are not the enemy. We are our best allies, and it is vital that you find women with whom you can share your professional journey. I am fortunate because my soul mates share my personal journey as well. In addition to a nuclear family, I have an extended professional family that includes my mentors, my mentees, and African American men in the academy. (Note that African American men also are not the enemy.) This network of professional friends turned family is a wonderful source of support and wisdom. I spent too many years suffering in silence, and I hope that my sisters at the dawn of their careers will understand that they do not have to "go it alone" and will keep an eye out for opportunities to develop mutually supportive relationships.

Like you, I have strengths that are in various stages of development. I always play to my strengths, which is my best tool for growing in confidence. Confidence, I believe, is an essential strategy for career success. However, I discover new strengths by challenging myself to try new experiences that exceed my comfort zone. Early in my career people extended professional opportunities to me on a national level and I would accept—not knowing that it was "too early" for me to be in those roles. Admittedly some of these opportunities came because I was among the few visible people of color since I was unknown in the field. My mentors never told me I would fail, and I took their various invitations to participate as a vote of confidence in my ability. The combination of internal and external confidence enabled me to move toward success. I did not let negative expectations, especially on my part, set boundaries for my professional involvement. The evaluator in me seeks informal, as well as formal, feedback on the results of my work. I seek this criticism from those whom I trust to be constructive and fair in their assessment. This trek for continuous improvement promotes my growing self-confidence. I encourage you to be diligent but deliberate in seeking those who will give you the truth and will give you the truth in a way that you can accept it.

Many years ago I had a professor who observed that I looked particularly worn and indicated that he had many responsibilities and was much older than I, but was not as worn as I appeared to be. My retort to him was, "You have a wife!" My point was that he had someone who could help him manage his life. I carried this principle over to my career and found help for managing my life. After all, I conceded that I am not Wonder Woman. After acknowledging I needed help I then gave careful thought to the kind of help I needed at the most basic level. For example, I discovered that I could pay for my home to be cleaned for about the same price as dinner and a movie. I discovered that sitting in a car wash was time well spent because for a few minutes I could mentally escape to a quiet place. The dry cleaner is my very good friend because it frees 15 minutes in my day. Taking the time to discover how to manage life more efficiently continues to be a tremendous benefit because it gives me the gift of time.

Dr. Carolyn Thompson told a group of young African American women, "You cannot live your life in fight mode; you have to pick your battles." Her words changed my life in a profound way because they enabled me to reason that if I can pick my battles then I have power. It changed the way I looked at the universe and my place in it. It moved me from being the victim to being the victor. I started choosing when to go to war and when to be at peace. The payoff for this change in thinking was a surge in energy that I could not have imagined. My newfound power changed my perspective in another way as well. I discovered what two-year-olds around the world know—the word *no*. Some battles are not always human confrontations; they also come in the form of overextending yourself simply because you think you must say *yes*. I have this *no* thing down to a science. I evaluate situations to determine the probability of value to me and the probability that I can add value for someone else. If the answer is no to either criterion, then I give it more thought. However, if the answer is no to both criteria, then the answer is no. Sometimes opportunities can lend tremendous value to me and others, and I still say no because the time is wrong. I know the limits of what I can do well and will pass an opportunity and hope that it will present itself again in the future. Be warned; there is an art to saying no in a way that does not alienate, embarrass, or devalue people. Take the time to learn how to say no in a way that will not force you into fight mode in the future. Selectively declining tasks enables me to know where to focus my creative and physical energy and is likely to do the same for you.

There was a time when my life was my career and I was frantically juggling research, teaching, and service. Whenever I was juggling, my whole world was turned upside down. Balance in life—as in career—is essential for longevity and sustained sanity. I continue to take the time to develop and participate in interests beyond career demands. Living as a one-dimensional creature is unnatural, especially for African American women. We are by nature multidimensional, capable of making meaningful contributions to many facets of life. Yet there is something about pursuing a career that frequently leads African American women to think of themselves as cheating if they are not consumed with work. You must—you absolutely must—find ways to bring balance to your life. I strive daily to work to live—not live to work. I fully expect to outlive my work years and believe that it is important to find meaning in living that will ground me during employment and will invigorate me in retirement. You have an advantage, since you can attain and maintain balance in life by design at the start of your career, which will enrich all your roles in life.

Spirituality is essential to my being, but my beliefs and values took a hit as I continued my role as gerbil. The "hurry up and wait" seesaw of the tenure process chipped away at me in ways that my training, mentoring, and work experiences did not prepare me for. I regained my internal locus of control and my sense of value by reconnecting to my own spirituality. It would be fair to say that my longevity in a career that frequently overflows with negativity and hostility is due to my spiritual development. I dare not prescribe a means for pursuing spirituality because this is a personal and private journey. I do encourage you, however, to find your own means of developing your spirituality. It is my spiritual self that finds calm in the midst of storms and finds hope for the future. Having a well-developed spiritual identity enhances my ability to see my purpose, particularly when people are challenging my right to pursue my career goals.

Someone once told me that laughter is good for the soul. The early days of my career did not present many opportunities to laugh; not much was funny. I made regaining my sense of humor as important as getting published. I placed laughter on my daily agenda and usually at the beginning of the day. Some days I go after the hunt for a chuckle with the same planned resolve as those on a safari. I do not grow weary of the hunt because the prize (a chuckle) is as necessary to my well-being as are food, water, and air! Laughter, early on, was not in my career because not much about seeking tenure is funny. The mental, emotional, and even physical release that comes through laughter still gives me a brighter perspective on the demands of the professoriate, making the hunt for laughter worth the effort. I now have almost predatory skills at finding the humor in many situations, including career-related matters.

This book documents that being a Black woman in the educational process is not easy. However, hope is presented here—evidenced by those who have transitioned successfully through the education pipeline. I hope my experience will give you ideas as well about how to manage your life beyond the classroom. Seek out and be selective about African American women who can become your family. Play to your strengths and never let anyone make you believe you do not have value. Control your workload as best you can by declining assignments or seeking help. Make your spiritual development as important as your professional development. Keep your sense of humor and seek balance in your career. More important, seek balance in your life by keeping your professional life in proper perspective. A dear friend of mine and I have a saying: "It's just a job." We chuckle and use this phrase to remind us that there are things in life that are just as important as work, or even more important. I urge you to remember that as you continue on your professional journey!

EDITORS AND CONTRIBUTORS

Benita J. Barnes is an assistant professor of educational policy, research, and administration at the University of Massachusetts Amherst.

Carolyn Buck is a STEM transfer specialist with admissions and records at California State University, Bakersfield.

V. Barbara Bush is an associate professor of higher education in the Department of Counseling and Higher Education at the University of North Texas.

Adrienne D. Dixson is an assistant professor in the School of Teaching and Learning, African and African Studies, Women's Studies at The Ohio State University.

Kassie Freeman is interim president of the Southern University System

Crystal Renée Chambers is an assistant professor in the Department of Educational Leadership at East Carolina University.

Marybeth Gasman is an associate professor in the Higher Education at the University of Pennsylvania.

Wynetta Y. Lee is a visiting professor in the Executive PhD. Program in Urban Higher Education at Jackson State University.

Venice Thandi Sulé is a research fellow in the Center for the Education of Women at the University of Michigan.

MaryBeth Walpole is an associate professor in the Department of Educational Leadership at Rowan University.

Rachelle Winkle-Wagner is an assistant professor of Higher Education in the Department of Educational Administration, College of Education and Human Sciences at the University of Nebraska, Lincoln.